KREMLIN KAPERS

KREMLIN KAPERS

ADVENTURES BEHIND THE IRON CURTAIN DURING THE COLD WAR

John A. Fahey

B & J Books
Virginia Beach, Virginia

B & J Books

P. O. Box 4511

Virginia Beach, Virginia 23454

ISBN 0-9679530-2-2

ACKNOWLEDGEMENTS

Ed Bacon and Ed DeLong of the Virginia Beach Writers Group -
Ed Bacon, retired editor of <u>The Virginian-Pilot</u>, for lending me his
editorial skill and Ed DeLong, author of <u>Mustang</u>, for his
encouragement and support. My wife, Barbara, for the many
corrections made in the final proofs. Marian Harris of the Virginia
Beach Institute for Learning in Retirement for her creativity in
choosing a clever title for this book.

All photographs were taken by the author except the photo of
John Fahey and Joseph Brodsky on page 188 which was taken by
the late Kevin Mulligan who was on the staff of Old Dominion
University's <u>Mace & Crown</u>.

To all the Old Dominion University Russian language students and Hampton Roads residents who toured the Soviet Union with me between 1972 and 1988. Thanks for some great memories!

Contents

Chapter One

Getting into the Soviet Union on the Backs of Injured Seamen

After a two year assignment as an American liaison officer in the Soviet Army stationed in East Germany, an exciting experience of spying covered in my book, *Licensed to Spy* , I spent one more year in the U. S. Navy before retiring from active service. After I retired from Naval service, I entered the public educational field and soon joined the faculty of Old Dominion University, teaching the Russian language.

Dealing with intelligence, spies, and Soviets did not end with my retirement in 1963 from the Navy. In the late 1960s and early 1970s one large Soviet fishing fleet from Riga, USSR fished off the Virginia Capes. The Soviet Union had a critical need for fish and protein. The USSR also had a need for intelligence. The Riga fishing fleet used the liberal United States recognition of international waters (beyond 3 miles) to come within the twelve mile territorial limit recognized by many other countries, including the Soviet Union. The close proximity of the fish factory ship, equipped for communications intelligence as well as fish processing, to naval and other military targets, enabled the Soviets to collect a wealth of intelligence information. Radars, including band width, frequencies, and other characteristics were major targets. Interception of military communications was also high on the priority list.

On February 28, 1969, a Friday evening, television news announced the transfer of a Soviet seaman from a fish factory ship to the U. S. Naval Hospital in Portsmouth, Virginia. The same night I received a telephone call asking me to assist an eye surgeon who would operate on the injured Soviet on the following Monday morning. I agreed, saying that I would visit the man the next day to become acquainted with him before the operation. On Saturday morning I left home for a foreign language conference at the Virginia Beach Cavalier Hotel and informed my wife that I would go directly to the hospital in Portsmouth around noon. When I left the conference, rain threatened, so I decided to stop at my home on the way to Portsmouth for an umbrella. Barbara told me that she was glad that I returned home because a Navy official called and asked her to tell me not to go to the hospital. He said that the injured man was an extremely sensitive individual. My wife was advised that no one outside active duty personnel would be allowed to be in contact with him.

The weekend newspapers headlined the arrival of the Russian seaman. On Monday the president of the Old Dominion University's Russian Club, Ms. Suzanne Beane, informed me that she was going to seek the hospital's permission to visit the Russian patient. During many telephone calls to the hospital throughout the day permission was denied. Finally, late on Monday afternoon, the hospital relented. A stipulation was imposed. Only two students and a university professor would be allowed to see the Russian patient the next day, Tuesday.

I selected an attractive young Russian language major, Kathy Gammil, to accompany Suzanne and me to the hospital. Both women were fairly fluent in speaking the Russian language. It was obvious upon arrival that the hospital administration was not happy about our visit. We were told that a naval officer would escort us to the patient's room. He would wait to see if the patient, Albert Kramarenko, agreed to the visit.

A lieutenant commander led us to the room. There was no sign that the hospital administration recognized me, a Old Dominion University Russian professor, to be the retired U. S. Navy commander contacted on Friday.

Albert Kramarenko was seated in his room with a visiting patient. Someone had found a guitar for him and he was singing. He looked up as we three appeared at the door.

"Albert," I said, "Take the young ladies' coats."

He hesitated at the word, "Albert," but when he saw the two gorgeous young ladies, he quickly jumped up to take the coats. The other hospital patient cleared out of the room. I shook hands with Mr. Kramarenko, a handsome man about thirty, and introduced myself as Ivan Ivanovich. Albert's hands were smoother than mine. This was no deck seaman!

We chatted, then sang, joked and laughed. Finally the lieutenant commander guard disappeared from the doorway. We were with Albert almost three hours when he asked if I would be willing to find the doctor so that he could learn his prognosis. Albert added that he had only one visitor during the weekend, a Navy captain who spoke Russian and questioned him. The doctor wasn't present at the time.

Urged by Albert, I was able to have the doctor paged.

Ophthalmologist Commander Davis arrived and at once shouted, "Do not lower your head!"

I repeated his words in Russian.

Davis said, "Thank God, you speak Russian. Please give him this list of instructions."

Dr. Davis provided a litany of cautions and told me that Kramarenko's eye was now sewn together like a jig saw puzzle with 88 sutures. Aboard the fishing vessel Kramarenko was sawing through a piece of black plastic when he snapped it to break it in two. A fragment flew into his eye.

Albert asked for his prognosis. The surgeon informed him that it would be a long time before the result of the operation would be known. Both Dr. Davis and Albert asked if I could return every day to assist them with the language barrier. I agreed on the condition that I could bring two of my students each day.

For about thirty days we met, sang, and talked. Albert opened up to me more each day. I suspected at first that he was at the very least a radioman, but as time went by, I believed that he had a more responsible position. He didn't admit to his specific duties until I tried a different approach. One of my students was a ham radio operator who spoke to Russians in the USSR at night.

"Albert, I am going to bring with me an experienced amateur ham radio operator who even speaks with your people in Russia."

"Fine."

"There is no one more expert in radio communications than my Mr. Dorsey. He's great!"

"I'd like to meet him."

"It may not be much fun. He's an amateur, but he's always talking shop about frequencies, interference, and so forth. You may not understand him or be bored."

"He's an amateur?"

"Yes."

"I'm a professional!"

That broke the ice on Albert's duties. Slowly but surely I learned that Mr. Kramarenko worked in a space that only he and the vessel's captain could enter. I found out that the Navy's Dam Neck firing range was the dividing line between the operations of the Soviet fishing fleets based in Riga, USSR and Cuba. Every day I learned more about the fish factory ship's capabilities beyond processing the catch. I never pressed Albert for information, but we became such close friends that he voluntarily told me about his life and duties aboard the ship.

He only knew me as Ivan Ivanovich. I knew him as Albert although I suspected that his first name might have been Alexandr. The four Russian letters for "Sasha," a diminutive for both masculine, "Alexandr," and feminine, "Alexandra," were tattooed on the four fingers of one of his hands. Sasha is one of the few Russian diminutives used by both males and females. He seemed to be happily married to his wife, not named Alexandra. I am sure that she didn't sit across the table from him at breakfast facing fingers with a girl friend's nickname. The tattooed letters must have represented his own name. His real name had to be Alexandr, not Albert.

On occasion during my visits Albert received telephone calls from the Soviet embassy. Even hearing only his side of the conversation, it was obvious that the embassy did not want me around him. He tried to assure the Soviet embassy that I was not a problem. He insisted that I only helped him and Dr. Davis. The USSR wanted him to return to his ship and except for Dr. Davis, the hospital administration seemed anxious to have him returned by the U. S. Coast Guard as soon as possible. Dr. Davis wanted him to stay because it was too soon to remove the sutures. Albert would have to endure the discomfort of blinking over 88 sutures until the fishing fleet returned to Riga in about two months.

Both the USSR and USA agreed to return him back to his parent ship before the sutures were removed. Despite the fact that the USSR wanted him out of the United States as quickly as possible, the Soviet embassy demanded that he have a new picture for his passport. Albert informed me that the hospital would not help him obtain a passport picture and asked for my assistance. I found a hospital public relations photographer who had a Polaroid camera. I convinced the photographer to work with me and take several photos until we got the exact same size of Albert's head as that in the photo to be replaced. Albert also needed a large bag to carry the toys and gifts sent to him by local residents who read about his family in the newspapers. I couldn't get a duffel bag in the hospital so I ran to a secondhand store in Portsmouth and bought two suitcases for him. I arrived back at the hospital out of breath as the Coast Guard and immigration officials entered his room. On March 18 the U. S. Coast Guard flew him to the fish factory ship.

Late at night, on March 27, my telephone rang. It was Albert. The Coast Guard flew him back again, after Albert complained of sudden severe pain in his injured eye. The U. S. Naval Hospital duty doctor refused to call Dr. Davis at home. He wanted Albert to wait until CDR Davis arrived in the morning. Albert insisted on making a phone call to me. I telephoned Dr. Davis who rushed to the hospital. Albert's eye was hemorrhaging. The next day Dr. Davis thanked me for calling him at once.

The second hospitalization provided the time necessary to remove the 88 sutures. Dr. Davis asked me to play a major role in their removal. He said that they had to be removed carefully, but quickly. The sutures could not be plucked out. On command, Albert must move his head up, down, left, or right as Dr. Davis seized each of the 88 sutures with an instrument. To keep the pressure and shape of the eye constant, Dr. Davis would have to work carefully around the eye ball. Any mistake would result in total blindness in the left eye.

Dr. Davis said to Albert, "I can give you these commands, up, down, left, right directly to you in English as each suture is removed or I can give them in English to Ivan Ivanovich who will give each to you in turn in Russian. I prefer directly in English because of the immediate time factor needed between each suture's removal and the added confusion that might develop with the extra words. If you turn right when you should turn left, my instrument will pierce your eye ball. If either you or Ivan make a mistake, if Ivan cannot keep up with my commands or if you miss Ivan's Russian call, you will be in danger. If you decide to take the commands in Russian, both of you will play more critical roles than I in the procedure."

I hoped that Albert would choose to follow Dr. Davis' English commands, but he turned to me and, as he put his arm around me, said in Russian, "Ivan Ivanovich is my buddy. I'll listen to his directions in Russian."

The directions came from Dr. Davis as rapidly as machine gun fire. Albert moved his head 88 times the instant I gave him the order. I never felt so alert and focused in my life. I didn't watch Dr. Davis as he moved his instrument around Albert's eye ball, latching onto each suture and maintaining the eye's shape. This seemed to be a greater challenge than that assigned to Albert and me during the procedure. Albert's and my contributions were concentration and alertness, not skill.

Rejoicing after the 88 sutures were removed, the three of us acted like school children. Tears flowed from both Albert's eyes. My strongest feeling was relief. Albert hugged me and would have given me the whole intelligence "bundle." It wasn't necessary. He already had.

The Soviet authorities finally agreed that Albert should return home for recuperation. On April 8, 1969, Albert Kramarenko, certainly befitting his status in communications intelligence, boarded a Soviet IL-62 airplane at Kennedy in New York with Soviet World War II war hero, Marshal Vasili Chuikov who was returning to Russia from duty, representing USSR at the funeral of President Eisenhower. Earlier Marshal Ivan Konev had the honor of representing his country at the funeral of Churchill.

Albert was in company of one of the most powerful figures in the Russian hierarchy. Marshal Chuikov was a member of the Central Committee of the Communist Party, a member of the Supreme Parliament, and twice decorated as Hero of the Soviet Union.

I learned later that the Navy captain, who visited Mr. Kramarenko when Albert first arrived, made a poor judgment call about Albert's status in the fishing fleet. After a conversation with Albert, he evaluated him as a deck fisherman. Shaking Albert's smooth hand alone indicated otherwise. Because of my past background as an American liaison officer assigned to the Soviet Army in East Germany where I was detained dozens of times and accused of espionage, all my requests for a visa to enter the Soviet Union were never honored. Maybe now things would change. At least now after a close relationship with Albert Kramarenko, I had one friend in the USSR.

Later another injured fisherman was transferred to the Public Health Hospital in Norfolk, Virginia. I was summoned to assist him.

"The Americans are trying to kill me," cried Soviet sonar operator, Konstantinas

Stankus, from the Soviet fishing trawler, "Saturn."

"No way," I replied as I approached his bed.

"Well they are going to let me die here."

"What's the matter?" I asked.

"Look!"

Mr. Stankus lifted the sheet. At waist level he and the bed were saturated with blood.

I tried to calm him, "It always looks like a loss of more blood than it really is."

He pointed out a large covered bowl on a table at the foot of the bed. I lifted the towel. The bowl was filled with large bright red cotton balls, completely saturated with blood. Waiting for the doctor to visit the patient, a nurse's aide had removed them from Mr.Stankus' stomach throughout the day.

"I am bleeding to death. I screamed when the bleeding increased every time they came in and raised me up to feed me."

I needed no more urging. The man had been bleeding profusely all day. No one had summoned his surgeon. I ran to the desk and had the surgeon or any other doctor available paged for an emergency. Fortunately his surgeon hadn't left for the day. Afraid to move him, the doctor worked on Mr. Stankus in the bed.

Konstantinas Stankus fell on a sharp object that penetrated his kidney. Russian fishing fleet doctors lacked the ability to stem the bleeding so on March 24, 1971 Stankus was evacuated to the U. S. Coast Guard cutter, "Point Brown," 30 miles southeast of Chincoteague, Virginia. He underwent an operation to repair the injury at the U. S. Public Service Hospital in Norfolk, Virginia.

The next day after the emergency surgery in his bed, I visited Stankus again. His spirits were high.

He said, "I felt like I was starving yesterday, but when the nurses raised my upper body to eat, I cried out, 'No.' They thought that I was not hungry and didn't know the bleeding intensified. Thanks for helping me."

We talked only about his injury. Before I left, I asked a navy retiree patient, Ed Wood, who occupied the room with Stankus, to watch out for him and not to let anyone raise him. Ed said that he had partially overcome the communication problem with hand signals.

I visited Konstantinas every day for the following two weeks. I learned about everything one could know about the Soviet fishing operation, crew morale, pay, techniques, and sonar equipment capabilities. Toward the end of the month Stankus told me that the hospital wanted him to sign his name to a document, but he didn't know what it concerned. He asked me to read it.

It was a release giving permission for an interview with the press. Checking into the reason, I learned that the Coast Guard wanted to arrange a visit with Stankus and the Coast Guard cutter commanding officer, Lieutenant (junior grade) Jeffrey Wagner, who evacuated him from the Soviet trawler. It seemed harmless enough, but the reporter was sure to ask Stankus lots of questions.

Stankus asked, "What should I do?"

"It's your decision. You don't have to sign the release."

"Can't I thank the captain without the press present?"

"Yes, but the U. S. Coast Guard public relations officer wants the press to be present. The U. S. Public Hospital will not allow the reporter present without your signed release. Think about it."

The next morning a representative of the Coast Guard telephoned me, asking me to convince Stankus to sign the release, recommending the interview as good PR for the Coast Guard and also Stankus. I offered my opinion that an interview with a reporter might not be in Stankus' best interest.

That afternoon Stankus again asked, "What shall I do? I want to thank the Coast Guard captain, but my country doesn't like publicity of any kind. I may get in trouble when I get back. Please tell me what to do. Should I sign the release?"

I advised him, "Sign, if you trust me. Everything that you say will have to go through me. I also will try to block any questions from the reporter leading to answers which I believe would be unpopular with your government."

Stankus signed the release. On March 29 LTJG Wagner, Virginian-Pilot staff writer Al Wheless and photographer J. T. McClenny met with Stankus.

During the interview Stankus said, "I want to thank the American people for what they have done for me. I hope that there will be peace and friendship between the Soviet and American people. I offer a great greeting from the Russian fishing fleet to the Point Brown crew."

He continued with information about his daughters, the normal catch (150 tons) of his trawler during the 2 1/2 month cruise, and the pleasure the crew enjoys listening to American TV and radio programs. The reporter asked a couple of political questions which I refused to relay, advising Mr. Wheless that any answers would get Stankus in trouble back home. The reporter took the rebuff well. On March 30 an article and photograph appeared in the press. Stankus was pleased with the content.

On the day of my last visit, Mr. Edm. Kishkis, Soviet Embassy's Consul of the Second Secretariat, was with Konstantinas when I arrived. He said to me, "First using this opportunity I wish to express my appreciation for your care and attention to our seaman, my countryman, Konstantinas Stankus. We are indebted to you. I will send you gifts, books, anything you want."

"Please, don't send me anything. What I would like, you cannot give me."

"What is it that I cannot give."

"A visa to visit the Soviet Union. I have applied without success many times."

"I can do this. Apply again and it will be granted."

"Thanks, but when you review my history, you will not be able to issue a visa to me. I've tried for nine years to get a visa without success."

"Konstantinas and I are compatriots. We are Lithuanians. Your person-to-person humanitarian relationship with my fellow countryman was selfless. You will receive a visa to visit the Soviet Union and I will send you some books."

"We'll see on the visa. Thanks. I really don't need any books."

To my surprise I received a visa to attend a summer language course conducted by Moscow State University in Sochi, a resort on the shore of the Black Sea. On the same trip this visa permitted additional visits to Moscow and Leningrad. Following this educational venture, from 1972 until 1988 I made over a dozen visits to the USSR as a leader of University Russian study groups and as a representative of an American business enterprise. I never again experienced a problem in obtaining a visa to visit the Soviet Union.

Several books arrived in the mail from Consul Kishkis. These fictional stories were published in Soviet Republic of Lithuania. Although the books were written in the Russian language, all of them had an anti-Soviet slant, a lesson supporting the strong dominance of ethnicity over loyalty to the Communist state.

As well as offering my humanitarian assistance to Albert Kramarenko, I was interested in collection of information on Soviet intelligence activities. On the other hand, visits to Konstantinas Stankus focused only on efforts to help him during his medical ordeal. I had reached a watershed. The days spent with a "license to spy" were over.

Now I could finally enter the Soviet Union - on the backs of two injured seamen.

Chapter Two

Taking the Socialist Brothers Down a Peg

Arriving at our hotel in Volgograd, USSR, our first sight was of a bunch of cigar-puffing Cubans hanging around outside the front door. It reminded me of a scene years earlier when I served as a shore patrol officer in Havana. The thirty of us on an Old Dominion University summer study tour pushed through the putrid smoke into the Volgograd hotel lobby. Cubans, Cubans were everywhere. As others wrestled with their luggage, I left mine in the lobby and ascended the staircase to check on the assigned rooms. On the third floor it was a relief to escape the cigar odor which filled the stairwell. The cleanliness of the room supported the claim that the hotel was the best in the city.

Descending the narrow staircase, i encountered one of my students carrying two heavy old fashioned, well worn leather bags. Following her was a dapper Cuban male.

"Nancy! What are you doing?"

"Taking this gentleman's luggage up to his room."

"Why in the world are you doing that?"

"He told me to take them to his second-floor room."

I pushed myself against the wall to let her and the smiling Cuban squeeze pass me.   In a few minutes Nancy was back in the lobby getting her own bags.

"Nancy, don't take any of their bags upstairs for them. You are not a bellhop."

She nodded agreement. I thought to myself, "This is going to be an unusual stop on the tour, seeing the sights of the battle of Stalingrad and stepping over and around Cubans every day.

Out on the street I entered the most hostile environment that I encountered since conducting a reconnaissance trip ten years earlier to Dresden, East Germany when in the early 1960's I served as an American liaison officer in the Soviet Army. The citizens in Dresden were angry about the fire storm bombing of their city which left Dresden in ashes and killed 120,000 to 150,000 people.   Dresden was a German cultural art center without military installations and was becoming a haven for refugees fleeing from the East, making it impossible to access an accurate count of the dead. The venting of stored anger at the rare appearance of an American those days in Dresden was understandable. I myself couldn't understand the choice of Dresden as a 1945 military target.

Now in Volgograd I faced the same citizen rage. The survivors of the Stalingrad siege blamed the United States for delaying the second front, permitting the Nazi front to extend to the east, finally reaching and reducing their city of Stalingrad to rubbish.

Volgograd was a Soviet city outside the usual tourist itinery. To see an American was an anomaly in daily life on the streets. Our bus driver passed the word that both Cubans and Americans had arrived in town. I was bombarded with questions, denunciations and caustic remarks:

"Why are you here? You permitted the Germans to devastate our city. We won the war. You did nothing!" Your president purposely delayed the second front until we had the Nazis on the run."

I replied, "Wait a minute. I could counter your accusations, tit for tat, and among many other questions ask why you let us fight the Japanese empire alone, but I'm here with a large group of young Americans to visit one of the most revered cities in the world. I'm here to see a city and its glorious war heroes who stopped and reversed the onslaught of the Nazi beast."

Even though I knew the answers, I asked questions about many incidents in the Battle of Stalingrad to give the questioners food for thought and show them my keen interest in their city's history. Although this tactic worked, some then voiced curiosity about reports they had heard about a possible impeachment of President Nixon. The ensuing dialogues gave my Russian a good work out.

Back at the hotel another scene shocked me. The center table in hotel dining room displayed a huge Cuban flag. Cramped around the sides of the room were small tables with tiny American flags on each table. I sought out the hotel manager and asked him why the Cubans were honored by sitting at the center table with a gigantic

Cuban flag and we were relegated to little tables with miniscule American flags.

"You are our American friends, but these Cubans are our Socialist brothers."

"Do your Socialist brothers speak Russian with you as do I and many of my students?"

"No, but they are loyal brothers in the search for a better world."

"Is it too much to ask that they do not smoke in the dining room?"

"Yes. It is too much.   We love their wonderful Cuban cigars."

We ate dinner that evening and breakfast the next morning choking on the cigar smoke and boisterous Spanish whoops and hollers radiating from the center of the dining room.

Without luck, earlier in Moscow I had checked magazines and journals in several kiosks to find out whether the latest edition of *Soviet Women* had reached the newsstands.   Two weeks before our departure from Norfolk, I received a telephone call from Suzanne Beane, a former ODU student, then a doctoral candidate in international business at the University of California at Berkeley.   Suzanne informed me that she had just received a telegram from Russia informing her that she had won an essay contest, sponsored by the Soviet journal, *Soviet Women* .   As a result, in addition to a prize her essay would appear in the next edition of *Soviet Women* .

The topic was, "A person who is dear to me" and I was cited as the person Suzanne chose for her winning essay.

After breakfast I decided to search the local kiosks. Lo and behold there was a newsstand in the hotel. Among the many government published magazines was the latest edition of *Soviet Women* . Sure enough, there was Suzanne's essay with my name featured throughout the article. Suzanne not only praised me for encouraging her educational interests and personal development, she emphasized my successful efforts in establishing a Russian language major at the university and promoting Russian cultural activities at the university and in the community.

This was all I needed to take the socialist brothers down a peg. Nothing appears in SOVIET WOMEN that is not sanctioned by the Communist government. I could hardly wait for my next encounter with the hotel manager.

His smiling countenance greeted me at lunch. "How do you like your little cozy tables? They are not so bad, are they?"

"Mr. Orlov, have you seen the current edition of *Soviet Women* ?"

"No. I don't read women's magazines."

"Well, you might want to look at this one."

"Why?"

"Your government has featured an article about me in *Soviet Women* ."

"Impossible!"

"You think that I am lying."

"No. I mean 'impossible' in the sense of surprise"

"I hope that you will read the article and see how it stacks up with your selection of what group should be honored in the dining room."

By dinnertime it was obvious that Orlov obtained his copy of *Soviet Women* . Our group was seated at the central table with a large American flag, The USSR's socialist brothers were directed to the small tables.

The Cubans' shouts and screams resounded off the walls. Orlov was very discreet, but curt in his response to them, "You had your turn! Also no more smoking in the dinning room."

The America flag flew proudly at every meal until we left for Leningrad. After their initial outburst about the move to the small tables, the Cubans no longer seemed to care where they sat.

The socialist brothers were still hanging around the hotel front entrance when we departed. One yelled, "Adios, American amigos."

I responded in Russian, "Goodbye, Russia's socialist brothers." My reply had no impact. They knew no Russian.

Looking back as the bus departed, I had the same thought as when we arrived, "It is just like a hotel scene in Havana."

Chapter Three

How to Avoid Nude Bathing with Your Professor and Still Get an "A."

It was 12:30 a.m. A taxi waited outside the Ostankano Hotel in Moscow for a fare still inside the hotel. I peeked over the crowd of rowdies clustered around the rear left wheel of the cab. A man's body was lying next to the vehicle. At first I couldn't see his head. Stepping closer, I saw that his neck was tucked under and behind the rear left tire.

"What's going on?," I asked.

"We're taking bets."

"On what?"

"On whether the taxi driver sees him before he steps into the cab or whether he gets in and drives over the drunk. The odds are in my favor for even if he sees him, he may drive over him anyway."

I didn't wait to see the outcome. Nothing surprised me anymore. Inside the hotel a drunk, trapped in the inoperable cage elevator, was still screaming and waving his now empty bottle of vodka. He had now been caged inside the elevator like an ani mal for almost two days. Few of those ascending the stairs paid any attention to him. Now and then a passerby would shout back, "Molchitye!" (Shut up! in English)

I had arrived at the Ostankano Hotel three days before on my way to enrollment in a Moscow State university Russian language course to be held in Sochi, a plush resort on the shore of the Black Sea. The first night I waited forever trying to get waited on in the hotel restaurant. I finally realized that it would never happen until I, like the other customers, let one of the waitresses sit on my lap. After some kisses and hugs she took my order and pranced off to the kitchen.

The Ostankano Hotel was not an Intourist Hotel. Traveling by myself, it was the only hotel available to me. I was the only foreigner registered, if one could call it that. I showed up and was directed to a room on an upper floor. My stay was an eye opener.

I had studied the Russian language for over twenty five years. I had interrogated some Soviet defectors, served in the Russian army in East Germany as an American liaison officer, and now was a faculty member, teaching Russian at Old Dominion University. I welcomed the opportunity to mingle with the people freely on the streets. No one suspected that I was an American. I had mixed feelings about leaving Moscow, but I looked forward to an intensive language program in Sochi.

Flying to Sochi from Moscow was another unexpected experience. The captain of the Aeroflot flight strolled up the aisle on his way to the cockpit cheerily greeting all the passengers. There was an unmistakable odor of alcohol on his breath. Some of the seat belts were not adjustable which didn't seem to matter much because most passengers ignored them. Hard candy was distributed by the stewardesses from trays to help the passengers swallow and relieve pressure on their ear drums. Most gobbled them up before the plane left the ground. Airborne, wine was served to half the passengers. Later the second half of the travelers received their share of the wine. I soon learned why there was two shifts of wine service. The same glasses had to be used twice to accommodate the entire plane load.

At first glance Sochi reminded me of Nice, France. That is, until I saw the beaches. From the boardwalk to the water's edge the entire beach was covered with stones. The mass of humanity stretched out on the stones extended for miles in both directions. I strolled along the boardwalk photographing the bathers, young and old, fat and fatter. Gigantic women in two piece bathing suits were a sight to behold. People in bathing suits were not allowed off the beach and boardwalk so all bathers had to come fully dressed from their hotels even if the hotel fronted the boardwalk with no intervening road. Metal booths were provided to change clothes on the boardwalk.

Compared with Moscow, my accommodations in Sochi were luxurious. A magnificent open dining room on the second floor overlooked the boardwalk, beach, and Black Sea. The food was gourmet.

I asked at the desk, "Is there any place less crowded on the beach/"

"As a foreign guest, you swim in a special area for our party members and government officials."

"Where?"

"Walk through the park beside the hotel and then to the sea. You will find a fenced in area with beach umbrellas, refreshments, and sand with a paved area down to the water's edge. To enter just show your hotel pass."

It was a short walk. Inside the fenced area there was an attractive wooden booth for changing clothes. Few bathers were inside the confinement. In the classless society, the masses were squeezed together on a rocky beach and the elite basked in the sun in a private paradise. What a country!

Two days after arrival I reported to the school. Classes were held in a secondary school. Classes for Soviet children had already started on the 2nd of September. Our classes were in a separate wing of the huge, very modern, building. Without delay, we were tested for Russian language proficiency. Three other Americans, two college students, male and female, and an older male were enrolled and placed in the class for beginners. I was placed in the advanced class with several Japanese, two Austrians, an East German woman, a Dutch couple, and a mixtures of unidentified Asians. None had a decent fluency in the Russian language, but did comprehend and could respond to questions. Our professor was gorgeous. I'd have bet on her winning any international beauty contest.

On the first day there was no instruction. The teacher asked each student in turn questions about his/her background and other inquiries which seemed to me were designed to establish a personality profile on the student. This approach didn't surprise me because I was sure that having a group of foreigners in the program, the KGB wanted to have a dossier on each person. I decided to be extremely guarded in my responses.

The instructor questioned the East German woman, "Whom or what do you hate most in the world?"

Glaring at me the young woman, struggling with her Russian, replied, "I despise Americans. They have been killing innocent women and children in Viet Nam. These capitalists are the worse war mongers in the history of the world."

When my turn came, all waited for my reply to the question with obvious anticipation. I answered, "I hate orange."

The teacher followed up, "The color?"

"Yes"

"What color do you like?"

Noticing her attractive dress, I answered, "Green."

The instructor smiled and said, "Our tastes are similar. My favorite color is green and I never wear orange."

Hearing this exchange of banter, the East German was furious. She interrupted, "He was supposed to tell us whom he hates."

Our teacher replied, "No. He had a choice, 'whom or what..' He chose 'what.'"

The next day the Moscow State University dream boat professor called me aside and said, "I have to give you some recently published advanced Russian language books. You'll like these texts. As teachers we use them to brush up on complicated grammar and expressions. No one in the class has your level of proficiency. Follow along each day with the class. I'll call on you when no one is able to respond."

Each day the teacher became more friendly. In a short time she asked me to call her by her first name. "Alya," a diminutive of Alisa. This was followed by a request to call me,"Vanya," a diminutive of Ivan.

Alya was housed in the same hotel and on same floor as I. i discovered this one evening when by chance I walked by her room. The door was open and I saw Alya in a slip ironing her green dress which turned out to be only one of the two she possessed.

We attended class between 1:00 p.m. and 6:00 p.m. After the fourth session Alya asked me to meet her that night on the beach to go nude bathing. I thanked her for the invitation and told her that I was married. With a wedding ring on my finger she knew this.

Alya said, "You have a good knowledge of Russian proverbs, but you do not seem to know this one - 'When a man is seven kilometers from his wife, he has no wife.'"

"Alya, Russians also have a proverb, 'A husband loving a wife is wholesome, but a brother loving a sister is splendid.' You are like a sister to me. It would be no fun nude bathing with my sister."

One day later Alya persisted on an evening rendezvous and then gave it up.

During this early period at the school I had a constant shadow who was difficult to shake. He first appeared at a Soviet Symphony Orchestra concert , held outside in a walled in enclosure. Shostakovitz's son was the conductor. When I arrived at the venue, I thought that it would be mobbed with ticket holders. I was surprised to find less than ten in the audience. I sat in the far right seat in the front row. Far to my left there was an individual sitting next to the center aisle. A Dutch couple whom I had met sat in the back. I was listening attentively to the concert when I felt a tap on my shoulder. I thought, "Where did he come from. There was no one there when I sat down." Then I noticed that there was no longer anyone on my far left. He had moved to the seat directly behind me. This well dressed man began to speak to me.

"I understand that you speak Russian. Let's get together after the concert for a few drinks at your hotel. We'll walk back together."

I whispered, "I'm sorry. I promised that I would walk back to the hotel with a Dutch couple attending the concert and then spend some time with them. They speak

English, but no Russian."

He continued to plead for a meeting, but I silenced him, expressing my desire to hear the orchestra.

The following day I was sunbathing in the VIP fenced off area when the same man ambled up and sat beside me.

"Happy to see you, again. .We can have a nice chat," he said.

"I'm sorry we can't. I've been here for twenty minutes and if I stay longer in the sun, I'll get burned."

"I'll get an umbrella. I want to chat with you about your President Nixon."

"No. I've got to go. It's time to study for this afternoon's class."

"Why? You're the best student in the class."

Now I knew that he was KGB for sure and that Alya had to report everything.

"If I'm the best, it's because I study. Look forward to seeing you again sometime."

I had one more encounter with the obvious KGB operative before I left Sochi for Leningrad. I had tickets to attend a circus performance. Kio the great Soviet magician was the feature attraction. In order to have time to get back to my hotel, change clothes, and eat dinner in time for the 8:00 p.m. show, I had to leave the school and walk two miles back to the hotel. At 3:15 p.m. I told Alya that I planned to leave the school at 3:30 p.m.

"Vanya, no way. It is a strict requirement that everyone comes to school on a bus and leaves on the bus. You cannot walk back."

"Then I won't get back in time to eat dinner before the circus."

"I'm sorry, but leaving early is against regulations."

"Alya, I'm leaving. If the authorities are worried about me, they can find me at the circus tonight."

"Vanya, I must warn you. I'll have to report this right away."

I left. Half way on my walk to the hotel, I sighted my KGB friend approaching me from the opposite direction.

When he was abreast of me, I stopped him.

I said, "What a coincidental meeting! Maybe you would like to walk back to my hotel with me and chat a little."

He abruptly answered, "No thank you," and hurried on his way.

The next day Alya was not angry with me for leaving school early. She let me leave class, asking that I stay in the building. School for the Soviet students was in session. I showed up suddenly in some of the classes. it was great fun. The teachers thought that I was a supervisor.

I heard one teacher say to a colleague, "Why are all these supervisors of instruction always men? Why don't women have a fair chance in this society. Men, I hate them."

Although Alya had to report my departure from class on the previous day, she never spread the word to teachers in the school that I was one of her students. She got a chuckle when I mentioned some of my experiences among the Soviet public school educators.

The Austrian student led the collection drive to buy a farewell gift to Alya. Although most students contributed money for the gift, I declined. I always refused politely gifts of any kind from my students, a carryover from my Navy days when gifts or acceptance of any gratuity was discouraged. When the last class period finally arrived, the students asked me to present the gift on their behalf. After declining several times to present their gift to Alya, the leader persuaded me to do so for them only because no one else had the fluency in the Russian language to make the presentation meaningful. Alya claimed neither to speak or understand English or any language other than Russian, a declaimer that I doubted, but it was true that she never uttered a word in any language other than Russian.

I decided to return the advanced Russian books that were lent to me at the same time.

At the front of the class, I said, "This is a gift to you from the students in the class who asked me to relate to you their gratitude for your excellent teaching, patience and kindness to each of them. I also at this time would like to return the books that you kindly gave to me at the beginning of instruction. They were most helpful and I thank you."

I was startled by a burst of tears and shrieks from Alya. Then she ran out of the room into the corridor. The class was stunned and members began to ask what in the world had I done. I repeated to them my words in English.

Finally one of them said, "You better go out there and see what's the matter with her."

Alya was standing near the door sobbing. Tears were running down her cheeks onto her green dress.

"Alya, what is the matter? The class was just trying to show its affection for you."

Trying to catch her breath, she muttered, "It's not them. Ivanka, It's you!"

Calling me, Ivanka, indicated she was mad at me.

"Me? Why."

"The books were my present to you and you refused them."

"A present! I thought that to just let me borrow them until the end of the session."

"They were my gifts to you."

"Well, I am sorry. I didn't understand. Of course I will accept them. "

Drying her eyes she said, "You will? You didn't realize that they were my gifts for you?

"Of course not. Come back to class."

"When I give out the diplomas, I have a special merit award for you as the best student that we have ever had in this program."

When we entered the classroom, Alya had restored her composure. Every student face looked with curiosity and wonder at Alya and me, but there were no explanations given to them.

Alya handed out the diplomas and then gave me a medal - strangely made of wood, engraved with a special citation.

As she gave me the medal, Alya whispered, "Vanyusha, one evening left. Will you go swimming with me tonight."

Calling me, Vanyusha, Alya was using a endearing derivative of Vanya.

"No, Alya, but I'll make one promise to you. For the rest of my life I'll never forget you."

I have never forgotten Alya, nor have I forgotten how I avoided nude bathing with her and still got an "A!" Nor have I forgotten the two Soviet seamen whose severe injuries were responsible for my eventual entry into this strange land.

Public beach in Sochi

No sand. All stones

Metal change clothes booth

Guardian of the beach

Bathers waiting to buy grapes

Fenced beach for foreigners and Soviet VIP's

Chapter Four

How to Steal a Renoir
When No One is Looking

Soviet guards were everywhere in Russia - inside, outside, all around the town. Guards in the Soviet Union were soldiers, old women, and anyone else in between. At first glance they look mean, aloof, and full of dedication. That is until you know how to deal with them.

All the Soviet military posts were numbered. Military Post Number 1 was Lenin's Mausoleum. A military honor detachment was housed under the mausoleum. As an extra credit question in an Old Dominion University course, I would ask the students to find the USSR's Military Post No. 1. Students would exhaust every possible source. They would call local librarians who would turn to me for the information. Librarians pride themselves in having answers for all callers and would vent their displeasure toward me when I told them that my students would have to dig deeper. Some students would telephone the USSR delegation at the United Nations who would not give the answer because either they didn't know or thought the students were attempting to uncover some dark protected secret.

I visited Military Post No. 1 about a dozen times and viewed Lenin's body. After the viewing, the strict routine was to exit by the right side door of the mausoleum and proceed along a path to the end of the Kremlin wall. A visitor then reversed direction and walked along the outside of the Kremlin wall. The only entry into the area was passage through the mausoleum. To the left were graves of Soviet heroes, Stalin among them, and to the right on Kremlin wall were placards with information about heroes whose cremated remains were contained in the wall. Every visit to view the burial vaults in the wall brought back many memories. When assigned to the Soviet forces in East Germany as an American liaison officer during the height of the cold war, I had contact with two Soviet marshals who served as commander in chief of Soviet Forces in East Germany. Both were now buried in the wall. At one banquet Marshall Yakubovsky chided me for not keeping up with the many "down the hatch" vodka toasts. It is the Russian custom to eat fish when drinking vodka.

Yakubovsky would shout at me, "Drink to the Bottom! What are you doing? Letting those fish lie flat in your dry belly."

The other Soviet marshal, Ivan Konev, the rival of Marshal Zhukov and Chief Justice of the Supreme Court which sentenced former Stalin KGB Chief Laveni Beria to death, once paid heed to my advice during one of the many crises occurring behind the Iron Curtain. I always marveled at my opportunity to chat with him while his own officers avoided any contact with him, fearing him like the plague.

By far I had the most fun at the beginning of the walk along the Kremlin wall. A Soviet guard was stationed there to prevent visitors from deviating from the designed track. Year after year the posted guard looked like a very young teenager. Armed, he stood unapproachable, it would seem, like the guards at Buckingham Palace or the honor guard at the Tombs of the Unknown Soldiers. Except for me, everyone passed silently and cautiously by him.

My first words to him would be, "Zdraviya zhelayu!" This greeting was used among the Russian military. In earlier centuries it was the way officers addressed soldiers and later evolved into a common greeting among Soviet military. The expression on the guard's face would immediately change from impassive to surprise. I would then ask him about his home town or village. This question always brought an outflow of jabber. No longer did he pay any attention to others approaching his post. If there was something to steal of value, one could walk off with the loot. Alas, there was nothing in the vicinity but flowers on the graves.

But in Leningrad there were many things of great value. The Hermitage Collection of Art houses priceless objects of art. Seeing so many Hollywood films depicting so many successful ways to steal valuable jewels and paintings by outfoxing a maze of electronic beams and museum guards, I wondered how effective security might be in the Winter Palace and three other buildings which make up the Hermitage Museum.

At the time of my visits to the Hermitage in the 1970's and 1980's, the collections numbered more than 2,700,000 items. These included about 15,000 paintings, 12,000 sculptures, 600,000 prints and drawings, over 600.000 archaeological exhibits, 1,000,000 coins and medals, and 224,000 items of applied art.

What a task to protect priceless collections in the four hundred rooms open to the public! The guards must be the best trained in the whole world. But wait. The guard force is made up of old women, some in their eighties and nineties.

Lets check the possibilities of walking away with a prize. I would love to have a Rembrandt. There are 25 Rembrandt canvases, several drawings and a large collection of etchings. The canvases are located on the first floor, one floor above the ground floor in room 254. My favorites are "Flora," in which Rembrandt portrayed his wife as the goddess of spring and flowers and "Portrait of an Old Man in Red." Both are too large to cart away. The small painting, "The Parable of the Laborers in the Vineyard," is more suitable for transport, but I don't like it that much. Room 254 doesn't seem to be conducive to robbery. It's too small and there are always too many people present. And why are there no guards in the room? I'd rather work my caper in a room where I could decoy the guards. With no guards the room must be protected by other means. The presence of guards is a signal that guards are an essential element in protection of the treasure.

On guard protecting the collection of 19th - 20th centuries French art on the second floor, third floor up from the ground floor were elderly women who appeared to be in their eighties and nineties. The collection was exhibited in rooms 314 - 350 which were wide open compartments off a long cul-de-sac. The women seemed quick-tempered and mean and always ready to whack the arms or knuckles of a viewer who threatened a painting.

They spoke only Russian and forewarned their prey with a shout, "Rukami nye trogat!," meaning, Don't touch!" Woe to the visitor who did touch a painting. The nearest female guard would swing with all her might, shouting, "Ruki proch!," meaning "Hands off!" The eagle-eyed elderly patrol could spot a potential violator from afar. Despite my warnings to students accompanying me on study tours, always one or two would be smacked.

The were lots of French impressionists' works inviting a touch or two: four van Goghs in compartment 317, eleven Cezannes in 318, fifteen Gauguins in 316, thirty seven Matisses in 343-345, plus Monets, Renoirs, and many others. All were at eye level with no restraining rope between the painting and the viewer. There was always the temptation to place one's face extremely close to the work, resulting in a burst of anger from the aged sentinel.

From all appearances of the layout, If a scoundrel could sidetrack the female guard, the rogue could make off with a treasure. Henri Matisse's "the Dance," 105.5 by 154 inches, and his "The Dessert Harmony in Red," 71 X 86,5 inches, would be too large to take on a getaway. Paul Cezanne's "The Smoker," 36 by 28.5 inches, Vincent van Gogh's "The Walk," 29 X 36,5 inches, and Paul Gauguin's "Tahitian Woman With Flowers," 37 X 28.5 inches, were all fair game. My favorite, Auguste Renoir's "The Girl with a Fan" was still smaller, 19.5 X 25.5 inches, and located in compartment 320, half way between the corridor's dead end and an exit. If I were the culprit, I would have only one guard to lure away from her surveillance of the crowd of viewers. An accomplice would have to make off with the loot.

Without any malice in mind and with a snippet of kindness in my heart , I always lured the senior citizen guards from their assigned duty. The sight of these poor wretched old crones awakened a intense feeling of pity in me. They were on their feet all day, shrieking in Russian, striking offenders, with no one with whom to converse.

Looking directly at a guard, I would call out in Russian, "Kakaya krasavitsa!," meaning in English, "What a beauty!"

Although the woman would be standing with her back to the wall, she would look over her shoulder to see whom I was addressing.

I would continue in Russian, "It's you my beautiful lady!"

"Me? Go on. I'm passed my prime. I'm ninety one."

"It's your face and especially your eyes."

"Who are you?"

"An American admirer. Is Leningrad your home?

"No, I'm from a village, 'Luga.'"

"I've been there. It's about half way to 'Pskov.'"

"Has it changed? I left when I was a little girl to come to the tsar's city."

I would describe "Luga" which like all Russian villages hadn't changed much in centuries. Right then and there anyone could steal a Renoir. On one occasion during a similar conversation, out of the corner of my eye I saw one of the students in my study group laughing and moving his grubby hands up and down on the back of the nude in Degas' "Woman Combing Her Hair." I cut short the chat with the guard to move him away from the pastel. This incident and others convinced me that the museum operated no cameras in this section.

Stealing anything of course was a fantasy. The State Russian Museum also had a valuable collection of Russian art. Guards in this museum also were elderly women. When I visited, I found it less crowded than the Hermitage. The female guards sat and controlled the viewer with motions and glares. While in the Hermitage photos without flash were permitted, the Russian Museum banned all photography inside the building. With some flattery and persuasion I convinced one eighty five year old guard to let me photograph two 14th century biographical icons, one of St. Nicholas and one of St. George. I later had both enlarged to 16 by 20 inches and gave one print of the St. Nicholas framed icon to St. Nicholas Greek Orthodox Church in Virginia Beach and the other to St. Nicholas Roman Catholic Church in the same city. The St. Nicholas Greek Church has displayed the icon print inside the church for many years.

I still don't know whether these gifts were sufficient retribution for having dreamt of stealing a Renoir from one of the greatest museums in the world.

Head of the line to Lenin's tomb

Young soldiers on duty at Lenin's tomb

Winter Palace

Winter Palace Cupola

Rembrandt's OLD MAN IN RED

Rembrandt's FLORA

State Russian Museum guard

State Russian Museum guard in the Icon Room

Chapter Five

Hey Ma! I'm Calling from Anton Chekhov's

Yalta! The jewel of the Crimea! What a change Yalta was from earlier days in the Russian resort, Sochi. Although both cities are on the shores of the Black Sea, they are as different as day is from night. Yalta has far less beach area, but the beach is not crowded. At every turn one can find something fascinating. Visiting Yalta's wonderful Botanical Garden, I spotted a redwood tree, reminding me of when I was entangled in a free balloon near the top of one in California thirty years previously.

I asked the guide, "Where in Russia are redwood trees?

"Nowhere in Russia as far as I know."

"Then, how did this tree get here?

"It was a gift from the United States."

That was all I needed to know. I was well familiar with the history of Fort Ross in California. Russians who colonized Alaska eventually moved south and established a colony in northern California. Imperial Russia had claims on this territory in the early nineteen century. The Russian settlers endured hardships at Russia's Fort Ross for over forty years and abandoned the colony just before gold was discovered in 1849.

It was obvious to me the redwood was delivered to the homeland by Russians at Fort Ross sometime in the early nineteenth century.

Not far from Yalta is the settlement of Livadia. The main attraction in the area is the 58 room Livadia Palace which was the summer residence of the last Russian tsar and tsarina, Nicholas and Alexandra. The palace is a fantastic combination of Renaissance style with an Italian patio, entered through metal gates forged by Ural masters. Patio walls have windows decorated with tracery grills. Florentine lanterns hang from the arches. Below is a white marble fountain. The rooms in the interior of the palace are finished in colored marble, majolica, and mosaics with ornate chandeliers and huge mirrors.

During the Yalta Conference, usually referred to as the Crimean Conference by the Soviets since it did not take place in Yalta, from the 4th to the 11th of February 1945 President Franklin Roosevelt stayed in Livadia Palace. The conference was held in the beautiful marbled White Hall. A tour of the palace begins with a visit to White Hall where the heads of USSR, Britain, and the United States met to decide the final questions of division of Germany and Eastern Europe at the forthcoming conclusion of World War II. The Hall is dominated by a painting of the heads of state and key people in the delegations sitting and deliberating at a large table in the room.

The Old Dominion University Study Tour of Russian language students and members of the Hampton Roads community obviously enjoyed seeing the luxurious residence of the tsar and the site of the historical Yalta Conference. Everyone in the group was on his/her best behavior. This exemplary conduct was not always evident on the part of every student. Often keeping a maverick in line was more challenging than dealing with the Russians. There always seemed to be one in the crowd who required constant attention to prevent a faux pas or unpleasant situation. The offender seemed to be a person with a good sense of humor, but his pranks were out of line in the Soviet environment. Any individual problem affected the entire group. On one occasion a student accidentally left his passport in Kiev. Upon arrival in Moscow no one in the group was allowed to check in at the hotel until the passport was retrieved.

As leader of these study groups, I found the responsibility to be a twenty-four hour job. Over the years many of those on the tours more than balanced the few who caused problems. Mary Honeyhake, a resident of Norfolk, Virginia always was alert and of great assistance. Jim Spinks and Ed Boone, community leaders, who knew Russian were always helpful when they joined the tours. Students like Jon Smith and Richard Norton made the tours most enjoyable.

There were also a couple of "Deep Throats" in every study tour who reminded me of the Watergate affair. With all of this assistance I kept well ahead of those few who had the potential to create a problem or embarrassment. That is until our visit to another of the wonderful attractions in Yalta.

I certainly had fair warning about the need to watch carefully the behavior and antics of Jake. He was the class clown on the campus. When we arrived in Leningrad, we first toured Peter and Paul Fortress. I had warned students in our group not to photograph soldiers in the fortress. Taking pictures of military was strictly forbidden and violation could adversely affect our entire group. At the entrance of the fortress Jake saw four Soviet soldiers sitting on a wall and immediately whipped out his camera. I was right on top of him.

"Jake! Don't take a photo!"

Paying me no heed, Jake pointed his camera at the soldiers and said, "Say 'sir.'"

"Sir" is the Russian word for cheese and anyone saying it would frown instead of smile.

I chastised Jake who responded, "I didn't take the picture."

Thinking that I was out of earshot, he whispered to a friend, "I got it!"

From then on I kept a close eye on Jake until we arrived at Chekhov's House in Yalta. Anton Chekhov was my favorite Russian author. Most admired Chekhov for his plays, *The Three Sisters* , *Uncle Vanya* , and *The Seagull* . I think that he was the best short story teller in the world of literature. In my opinion he outdid O'Henry, Twain, and a host of others. To have a full appreciation of his work, one would have to have a good understanding of Russian life and the Russian language.

Chekhov suffered a lifetime of poor health and living with a dysfunctional family. Although full of physical agony, his happiest days from 1899 to 1904, the year he died, were spent on his plot of land in the village of Verkhnyaya Autka on the outskirts of

Yalta. Chekhov House has a treasure of objects associated with his life: a bronze casket, medals, souvenirs, and inscribed photographs from Leo Tolstoy, Pyotr Tchaikovsky and others. Everything in his study is kept as it was on May 1, 1904 when he left the room for the last time for the Badenweiler Resort in Germany where he died two months later on July 2, 1904.

Among the many prized objects in the house is an old fashioned telephone. In 1896 the first of Chekhov's best known plays, The *Seagull* was produced by the Imperial Theater in St. Petersburg. It was given a terrible review, so bad that Chekhov in bitterness vowed that he would never write a play again and left the country. Later Konstantin Stanislavsky's Moscow Art Theater, with its new method approach to acting, changing actors into real animated human beings from their former stilted, wooden characters, produced the play. Chekhov, ailing in Yalta, telephoned Moscow from Yalta after the opening performance to learn of the audience's reception to the Moscow Art Theater production. The old fashioned telephone on which Chekhov made the call is among the prized objects in the house.

As the twenty five of us slowly crept along the rather cramped spaces, the museum's guide paid special attention to the telephone on the wall. It was completely roped off. The guide was especially proud that over the eighty years since Chekhov left the house in 1904, no one had used the phone.

Having moved on after the guide said, "Anton Chekhov was the last person to place the earphone against his ear," we heard a booming voice from the rear of our group, "HI ma. I'm calling from Anton Chekhov's" It wasn't the ghost of Chekhov. It was that of Jake!

I was in front of the group close to the guide who was speechless with a look of horror on her face.

I hurried back to the end of the line to see Jake inside the roped off area with mouth close to the speaker and the ear piece next to his head. He was giving a Yalta weather report to his mother in Chicago.

"Jake, put the phone down and get out of there."

The poor museum attendant could barely speak as she pointed to the door. In good faith no longer could she finger Chekhov as the last person to pick up the phone.

I made a weak attempt to console her.

"At least no call has been transmitted on the phone since Chekhov."

I didn't give her Jake's name. I thought that I would spare her the thought of someone named Jake being the last one to handle the telephone.

The last description of Jake's performance from the guide was, "Uncultured."

I cautioned Jake about any future misconduct and kept my eye on him every step of the way until our return.

For a long time I could still hear his voice ringing in my ears, "Hi ma. I'm calling from Anton Chekhov's." It was a audacious, uncalled for, boorish act. But well aware of Chekhov's unmatched keen sense of humor, I know that somewhere above can be heard a chuckle or two from the former occupant of the house.

Livadia Palace

Conference painting in the White Hall

Tour members removed from Chekhov's House

Chapter Six

The Bear is Loose, but Don't Panic

Those not closely familiar with Russian lifestyle surmise that chess is the people's favorite board game and that ballet dancers are alone on the highest pedestal of Russian artists. Nothing could be further from the truth.

The most popular board game is dominoes. The game is played everywhere, in the military, in the factories, in the homes.

Figure skaters and circus performers are in the same prestigious artistic hierarchy in Russia as ballet dancers and enjoy the same privileged status. Yes, circus performers!

Just about every city in Russia has a circus building. Often the circus structure is the most attractive building in the city. In Moscow there are three sites in the city where one can see the circus. The newest structure is the building of the Moscow Circus, located near the Universitet Metro Station on Vernadsky Prospekt. It's a tent-like glass building, designed by architect, Yakov Belopolsky. This unique building which seats 3,400 spectators has a ring with four interchangeable floors, switchable within five minutes. One floor is an ordinary circus ring, a second for aquatic shows, another a rink for ice ballet and the Circus on Ice, and a fourth special ring for illusionists, like the Great Kio of the 1970s and 1980s. There are foyers with buffets which encircle the arena on two levels. In an additional building are a training ring, dressing room, stables, and exercising pens.

Two other opportunities are offered in Moscow to see the circus: The Old Circus on Tsvetnoi Boulevard and during the summer the traditional tent circus in Gorky Park.

St. Petersburg not only has a circus building, seating 2,465, but offers a Museum of Circus Art. The museum has more than 80,000 exhibits, including circus props, scale models of circus acts, documents, photographs, and literature on the history of the circus.

Circus is big in Russia. During two decades of visits to the Soviet Union, I saw just about every kind of circus offered. The Moscow Circus on Ice had bears playing ice hockey. The Moscow Circus in the Water had a diving bear. Bears are often featured performers in the Russian circus. Russian categorize animals, placing bears and elephants among the dumbest. Some believe that the bear is the national favorite in Russia, but the eagle is most admired. A fox is considered sly, but a rabbit is thought to be a coward. Russians have a proverb, "One can even teach a bear," meaning anyone can learn if a bear can.

I learned something at Russian circuses from a bear - not to sit in the front seat at the Russian circus. It happened in Volgograd at a performance of the Russian Circus in the Water. Everyone was seated waiting for the circus to begin. I was given a ticket in the first row. My students were spread around the arena. Before anyone appeared in the ring, screaming, loud shouting, and fierce growling sounds came from the back stage area. Minute by minute the noise continued at a higher crescendo. Finally, a man appeared running along the perimeter of the ring.

I stopped him and asked, "What's the matter."

"The bear is loose. Don't panic!"

I was close to the backstage entrance into the ring. I felt that I had a good reason to panic.

Finally the shouts and screams subsided. The growling and snorting continued. Then out comes the biggest bear that I had ever seen. I was thankful that he was led by a burly keeper. The bear had a muzzle, but his claws looked threatening. He passed two feet in front of me. I almost gagged from the obnoxious odor. Already I was willing to give up my prized first row seat.

During the bear's act when he dove into the pool, the water splashed all over me. i was drenched. As wet as I was, I was more afraid that the huge bear would climb out of the water and end up on top of me. The Russians may be right about bears being stupid, but I learned from one - never sit in the front row.

Despite this lesson, I found myself again in the first row when the accompanying Soviet guide gave me my ticket at a circus in Kiev. I sat glumly waiting for the first act. At least I thought, "It's a traditional circus. I can survive."

With five minutes before the scheduled opening, an ODU student, Bonnie, approached me, "Mr. Fahey my seat is behind a pillar. I can't see anything in the ring."

"Bonnie, take my seat and I'll sit in yours."

"No, Mr. Fahey, that isn't fair. You won't be able to see a thing."

"Bonnie, I've seen a lot of circuses. I don't mind a bit."

Bonnie couldn't believe her good fortune, a front row seat. I took her seat many rows back which was directly behind a wide column. To the left of me was an extremely attractive young woman. Chatting with her from time to time, I learned that she was an American with another tour group. I arranged a meeting for her with a very nice young student in our group.

When we gathered together again after the performance, I questioned Bonnie about her view of the circus.

"How was the seat?"

"It was great, Mr. Fahey, but my legs are covered with muck and dung."

"What happened?"

"It was the camels. The dirt floor in the ring became muddy and when the camels trotted by close to me, they splashed mud and camel dung all over me."

Bonnie wasn't upset about the dirt. She enjoyed the circus. I would have been upset had I stayed in the first row. It's one thing to be scared and splashed by a dumb bear, but to be splashed with muck manure by smart camels - that's asking too much.

Chapter Seven

Where's the Beef?

On almost every trip to the Soviet Union I visited a zoo. In the early 1970s Soviet zoos flourished. The Moscow Zoo, located close to the nearby American Embassy, was divided into the old zoo and the new zoo. Tickets were purchased at the entrance to the old zoo. After visiting the old zoo, one crossed a street and presented his/her ticket stub to an attendant at the new zoo.

The rundown old zoo housed the big cats, wolves, exotic birds, while the new zoo provided more comfortable spaces for bears and a multitude of other animals. The tigers in the old zoo were a pitiful sight. They were cramped in a cage with hardly room to turn around. One tiger had a bloody snout from rubbing his nose on the bars every time he turned his head.

As usual the bears were one of the main attractions, especially the polar bears. One was trained to stand upright and wave. Enjoying the sight of happy animals in the new zoo, one felt completely outside the Soviet environment.

Toward the end of the seventies and into the eighties, a complete change took place. The Moscow Zoo began to run down in appearance and quality. Russian visitors stood with children peering into enclosures waiting for animals to come out of their caves or housing. The Russians didn't realize that there were no more bears within the fenced area. I saw children standing for hours around the exhibits expecting animals to appear at any moment. What had happened?

The Soviet Union suffered a severe meat shortage during this period. Even in the best hotel restaurants, diners were told, "There is no meat."

Once I said, "O.K. There is no meat, Then give me chicken."

The waiter said something like, "You dunderhead! I just told you there is no meat. Chicken is meat."

For awhile the Soviet zoos in the beginning of the meat shortage did receive meat for the animals. But the meat never got to them. The zoo keepers took the meat home, causing a countrywide zoo scandal. Cartoons appeared in the press showing angry lions roaring as the zoo keepers departed with the beef, slated to be the lions' meal.

At this time somehow the notorious zoo in Karaganga got some piglets.

To the horror of parents in company with their children, the zoo keepers threw the live piglets into the cages to be killed and devoured for all to see. The Soviet administration admonished the keepers for their lack of discretion in feeding the animals during visiting hours. Eventually the Karaganda Zoo closed down for a long period. A fire had swept through the zoo's antiquated wooden cages and buildings. When the zoo was back on line, there was an attempt to restore its stature with the claim of having a talking elephant. This claim received international press coverage, proving the disinformation can be disseminated by Communists even with false disclosures in the lowly animal world.

Time permitting, when study group students were researching information for support of the required papers on assigned phases of Soviet lifestyle, I took a few community members in our group to the Moscow Zoo. With only three or four with me, we could ride the crowded Soviet Metro to the zoo. With the demise of many exhibits in the late 1980s the zoo offered little of its former appeal. Birds were still plentiful, but it was obvious that the friendly trained polar bear had waved his last goodbye.

In addition to the St. Petersburg Zoo with 360 species of animals, the city is especially proud to host the Academy of Sciences' Zoological Institute and Zoological Museum on the embankment of the Neva River. The museum's collections include over 40 thousand specimens of the animal world. The museum's "Hall of Mammoths" was touted during the Communist days as having the world's only stuffed mammoth on display.

Thankfully in this museum's zoological setting this question never arose, "Where's the beef?"

Circus Building in Sochi

Ground level floor Sochi circus building

Polar bear at the Moscow Zoo during the good times

Empty cage at Moscow Zoo

Chapter Eight

Sing Along

When I was a boy, I thought that I had a good singing voice. I sang in the choir at St. Joseph Roman Catholic Church in Medford, Massachusetts. Only a few schoolage children were selected as choir members. As we were singing on one Sunday, a nun appeared at an open door at the side of the choir and beckoned to me to come to her. I waited until the hymn was finished.

"You have to leave the choir right now!"

"Why, sister?"

"Because you don't attend parochial school."

I was disappointed, but not surprised. Earlier I studied and memorized the entire Latin language in the Mass in expectation of being an altar boy. When I thought that I was ready, I knocked on the parish rectory door.

Father Ryan opened the door, "What do you want, John?"

"Father, I've studied the Latin Mass and am ready to be an altar boy."

The response came quickly, "Sorry only students at our parochial school can be altar boys."

This rejection didn't deter me from taking Latin later in high school which piqued my interest in languages and led to an eventual career as a linguist. However I never tried to sing again. Even during the singing of hymns at our church today, I listen.

That is with the exception of Russian I don't sing. Teaching Russian, I found that singing was a valuable teaching tool. At Old Dominion University I taught my students the French song, *Frere Jacques* , which in Russian is *Brat Ivan*. It was great fun for all of us in class when the second, third, and fourth rows would follow the first row, stanza by stanza, everyone singing at the top of their lungs. A nearby French class (which never sang) would slam its door shut before we got to the third row. We also sang *America the Beautiful* in Russian, *Moscow Nights* , and some Russian folk songs.

In contemporary Soviet life there were many other songs which never reached the West. My favorite of all was also the favorite of the Soviet Air Force, *Pevym delom Samolyoty* , from the musical production, "Flying Sloths."

The tune was very catchy and the words clever. In the chorus when the pilots sing together that their first order of business is airplanes, someone shouts, "What about girls!" The answer, "Girls will be later," follows. In the 1970's it was among the top hits in Soviet society.

Visitors to Communist Russian usually returned with a view that Russians on the street were glum and unhappy. Russians look down and never recognized a passer by with a hello. You never hear, "Have a happy day!" Some foreigners think that the Russians drank to excess because their life was so hopeless under Communism. Nothing could have been further from the truth.   It was not a custom in Russia to say,"Hi" to every one you meet. Drinking was carried down from the days of the Tsars, through Communism, to the present socalled democracy. It has been part of Russian heritage and culture.

One of the easiest tasks in the world was to change the glum faces of Soviet pedestrians or public conveyance riders by song. Any time I rode on a crowded (They were always crowded.) bus or trolley, I would begin talking with the nearest male Russian who would without fail ask me where I lived in the USSR. When I said that I was an American, the excitement would begin.

He would shout to the other passengers, "We have an American who speaks Russian on the bus."

Everyone would pressed inward and ask questions: "Where are you from?" "Where did you learn to speak Russian?" "How many automobiles do you have?" "How much do they cost?" "How long do you have to wait to get a car?" "What do you do?" "How much do you make?" "Do Americans really want war with us?"

I would steer the conversation to the life in Russia and as quickly as possible tell the load on the bus, trolley bus or trolley how I loved their music.

"How many of you know *Pevym delom Samolyoty* ?"

"We all do."

I would start the first verse in Russian, "We are friends, migratory birds."

A few would join in the second verse, "Only one habit, only one habit is not good."

Far more riders would shout out the third and fourth verses, "On the earth we have not succeeded in marrying. And in the sky one cannot find girls."

Everyone then would holler, "Why?'

The whole crowded trolley car would then sing the chorus at the top of their lungs, "Because, because we are pilots. The sky is our, the sky is our native home. Our first business, our first business is airplanes."

At this point in the chorus someone hollers, "What about girls!

The trolley car voices boomed with the last line, "Girls will be later."

One could never entice a crowd in trolley car or bus in another country to join in such frivolity. The Russians were quick to enjoy what little good times that could be had between waiting in lines patiently for goods of all kinds. Their sense of good humor was extraordinary. A trolley full of boisterous singers led by an American raveling down the Moscow streets deferred any thoughts of animosity in the period of

he so called Cold War. Sing along diplomacy - it worked.

Chapter Nine

The White Crow

The telephone call was from someone in the Department of Defense asking me whether I would be interested in taking a position in Moscow at the American Embassy. If I was interested, my name would be submitted for consideration. Having made many trips to the USSR, I was not interested in permanent residence or employment of any kind in Russia. Had I had interest, I still would have been wary of being a candidate with a slew of others. I recalled a previous recommendation of a member of U.S. Information Agency that I be a candidate for chairman of the Foreign Language Department at the United States Military Academy. The USIA official with whom I had worked closely in Washington when I was Director of the Navy Language School was convinced that I was the best possible candidate for the position and recommended me highly to the Academy. I was told that my lack of graduate education at the time was no impediment because if selected, West Point would support a continuation of my education to the terminal PhD degree. I was a finalist in the process, but the selection committee made the proper choice, appointing an individual who already had a doctorate. Had I been selected, I would eventually change rank from commander, U. S. Navy to brigadier general, U. S. Army. What a kick!

My next phone call related to the same subject. The American Embassy revealed what the first call was all about. An employer of Grace Industries informed me that a Department of Defense contact recommended me to make a site visit to the U. S. Embassy in Moscow for the company. The Department of State was now going to turn over responsibilities for the maintenance of the entire new embassy complex: electronics, mechanical, janitorial, etc. to private industry. Grace Industries, Inc. was high up in consideration in the competitive process for the contract award. I learned that a site visit would involve a visit to the new embassy, now under construction, to gather all the information needed to make a competitive bid.

One of the company's managers was working on a Grace Industries job at the Little Creek Naval Amphibious Base so I made an appointment with him to learn about intricacies of the site visit.

I asked, "What qualifications do you want for this job? I'm not an engineer."

"We heard that you speak fluent Russian and served on Navy intelligence assignments. We need to know what cost is involved in maintaining the complex. There are three American companies now on the site. What are they paying workers in per diem to live in Moscow? What will be involved in removal of snow from the roof? We need to know about the generators, the electronic equipment, and everything that will relate to the cost of maintaining the new embassy."

"It sounds like a challenging venture. I'll go."

"Let me know tomorrow what you'll charge for up to ten days in Moscow on the job."

A week later after I informed him of my fee and was told the visit was approved, he told me that Mr. Grace wanted to see me.

"Mr. Grace now believes that he can make a bid without a site visit, but he'll talk to you briefly this morning."

Arriving at the office of Grace Industries in Hampton, Virginia, I was asked to wait in the reception room. There were certificates and photographs on the wall which revealed that Mr. William Grace was a Republican, an African-American, and, as I recall, had some sort of a connection with President Reagan. In about ten minutes I was led to Mr. Grace's office.

Mr. Grace greeted me warmly, but gave me some bad news.

"I think that we can make this bid for the contract at the U. S. Embassy in Moscow without a site visit. I hope that we haven't caused you any inconvenience."

"Mr. Grace, I have rearranged my entire schedule to leave on this trip. I had all sorts of commitments that I had to postpone or cancel."

"I'm sorry, but this is business and things change. Your personal life is important, but doesn't override business considerations."

I was really upset, but I realized that I was not going to get anywhere pleading my inconvenience. I decided to take a different approach. I had read closely the detailed specifications for making bids for the contract.

"Mr. Grace, you said that you believe that you don't need to send anyone to Moscow for a site visit before making the bid. This is contrary to the requirements to make a bid which state clearly that all bidders must make a site visit to the new Embassy.

"Well, I don't think that I will need one."

The first thought that occurred to me was that it was divined already that Grace Industries would get the contract. It would make sense. Grace Industries was a front runner in maintenance around the world, having current contracts with the federal government in the Middle East and at the Naval Amphibious Base in addition to work in the commercial area, including K-mart. What a cultural coup it would be for President Reagan to show off to the Soviets how successful an African-American firm can be in America, the land of the free.

"Mr. Grace you may think that you have the bid in hand, but things change in business. The fact that you did not make a site visit as required may make your bid vulnerable. I'm not an engineer, but I am hard working and I know the Russians. I'm confident that I can provide information which will enhance your bid."

Mr. Grace thought a moment and then said, "Well, thank you. See my Little Creek manager tomorrow. He will have my answer."

The next day I was told to go to Moscow. I immediately visited the Garris Travel Service in Norfolk to arrange for the trip to Moscow and requested that the agency seek accommodations for me at the National Hotel. I had never stayed there with my

ODU study tours, but did dine there on several occasions and found that the hotel served the best food in Moscow. While at Garris, I called Grace industries to request an account be established at the agency so that my air fare and Moscow lodging could be charged directly to the firm and not to me. In this manner I could limit my final invoice to meals and my fee. Getting a visa with the help of the Department of State was easy because my visit to Moscow was considered to be an official one on behalf of the government.

After a good night sleep at the National Hotel in Moscow, I decided to walk from the hotel, located near Red Square, to the American Embassy. Stopping to observe the crowds waiting for the stores to open and chatting from time to time with Russians on the street, it took about an hour and a half to arrive at the Embassy. The secretary to the Counsel for Administrative Affairs, Mr. David Beale, checked my name on her list and advised me to return to my hotel to await a call from her arranging an appointment with Mr. Beale.

"When will you call?"

"I don't know."

"I assume sometime today."

:"Not necessarily. It may be tomorrow or toward the end of the week."

"Wait a minute! I'm being paid to do a job here. I cannot wait around all week to begin my site visit."

"You will have to wait. Mr. Beale is new on the job and has lots of things to take care of. Please go to your hotel and wait for a call."

"For the money that I'm being paid by Grace Industries, I'm not going to sit by a phone in my hotel room and wait for a call. When Mr. Beale is available, please try to reach me at the office of the Senior Military Attache which must be somewhere in this building."

I left the office and asked the first person I saw to tell me where the military attache was located.

"On the top floor somewhere in the back of the embassy."

"How do I get up there?"

"There's an elevator somewhere back there."

In the back of the building I found what appeared to be a freight elevator. It was a rickety contraption. I decided that this must be it. I found a button to push and up I went. I kept my finger on the button until the elevator reached the top and stopped. In front of me was a reception room, a desk manned by a young Marine, and a comfort-able couch.

I said to the Marine, "I'm here to see the senior military attache."

"I'm sorry sir. He's with the ambassador."

"That's all right. I'll wait here. Let him know that he has a visitor when he returns."

"Sir, I don't know what time he will get back."

"I'm in no hurry. I'll just sit here and wait."

Only ten minutes passed before Rear Admiral Ron Kurth practically flew into the room.

"Admiral, you have a visitor waiting to see you."

The admiral turned to me, "I've got something to do for the ambassador right away. Could you wait ten or fifteen minutes?"

I thought, "Could I? You bet," but I answered, "Yes sir. Thank you."

As I waited, I wondered if Admiral Kurth would remember me. A few years ago we had met at a social affair held by a mutual friend, Paul Lasko, a former assistant naval attache in Moscow.

In less than fifteen minutes the Admiral Kurth returned and asked me to follow him through the steel door to his office.

"Have we met before?"

"Yes sir, at Paul Lasko's home in Virginia Beach."

"Nice to see you again. Can I help you with anything?"

I began to explain the nature of my visit and present difficulty in seeing the Embassy's counsel for administrative affairs. Admiral Kurth was very hospitable, asked me to join him in a cup of coffee, and listened to my tale attentively.

Finally he said, "The counsel is new and won't have a lot of information of value for you. You've got to talk to the contractors. The general contractor of the project is a Soviet construction company with three small American firms responsible for specialized tasks, like electronics, mechanical, heating, etc. First try to find the American foreman who is a liaison with the Soviets and the three American concerns. Take a look at the new complex."

From Kurth's office window, I could see far down below the entire new embassy buildings. Workers who looked like ants were scurrying around the grounds.

The admiral continued, "Go to the FBO security gate at the new site and ask for Sid Goldberg. He is under contract with FBO. He is the most knowledgeable individual on the site." I understood FBO to stand for "Fixed Base Opera tions."

Suddenly all the lights went out and at the same time the phone rang.

The admiral said, "Another loss of power. It happens several times a a day."

Answering the phone, he said. "Mr. Beale's secretary has been trying to reach you before you left the grounds. You have an appointment with the counsel at 4:00 p.m."

"That means I have about five hours to see what I can find out before I see him.. I'll try to see Mr. Goldberg."

After thanking Admiral Kurth, I left to find Mr. Goldberg. At the security gate to the new embassy I encountered Mr. Barney Bell who was having trouble with a drunken Russian worker who was trying to leave the site without surrendering his pass. I soon learned that no one manning the gate knew sufficient Russian to communicate with the workers. I offered my assistance which was appreciated and the drunk gave up his pass.

I then said to Mr. Bell, "I would like to talk to Mr. Goldberg."

"I'm sorry, but without authorization, I cannot let you into the site."

"Could you summon Mr. Goldberg to the gate?"

"I'll try to get him."

In short order Mr. Goldberg arrived. I apologized for calling him off the job, but he didn't seem to mind. I explained my need to learn everything possible for Grace Industries to make a competitive bid for the contract.

Mr. Goldberg replied, "You will get a detailed tour of the site, probably tomorrow. I would advise you to contact the American project managers beforehand. They will not come to the gate, but in about fifteen minutes you may be able to corner the three of them at lunch in the commissary."

His advice was good. At the commissary I found the three project managers and obtained their office locations in Moscow, all within walking distance from the embassy. I made good use of the afternoon before my 4:00 p.m. appointment with Mr. Beale.

I decided to nail down the per diem paid to the workers by the three American contractors. When I approached the building where the FBO was located, I was blocked by a Soviet policeman. He asked to see my passport and visa. Immediately a problem arose. Despite a State Department letter (which I never saw) explaining the site visit and U. S. sponsorship in order that I would receive a business visa, the visa that arrived on August 9 before my departure stated that the purpose of my visit was "tourism."

"What are you doing in this area? There is nothing for tourists here."

"I am on official business to visit the Department for Construction of the U, S, Embassy."

"You have no authority to do so. You are here as a tourist.."

"It's a mistake. You know it happens all the time."

"Well, it's also your mistake to come here off the beaten tourist track."

Aware that a large number of people in Moscow are from other areas of the Soviet Union, I asked him, "Where is your home town."

"How do you know that it's not Moscow."

"By the way you pronounce your "O."

"I'm from Kiev"

"Kiev! My favorite Soviet city. It's a 'green area.'"

That's all it took to get him talking. Calling a city a "green area" is the highest compliment possible. With parks and magnificent grounds, Leningrad always claimed to be greener that other cities. The Leningraders didn't pay much attention to Kiev because Moscow was their big rival. However, Kiev paid close attention to all the other cities.

"Have you ever been to Kiev?"

"Many times. I told you it is my favorite."

Testing me, the policeman responded, "Well, tell me what you like about Kiev."

"There are so many things to like: The Golden Gates at the corner of Vladimirskaya and Yaroslavov Val streets, the wonderful 11th century monument, surrounded by a picturesque garden; the grandeur and splendor of St. Sophia Cathedral, containing the marble sarcophagus of Yaroslav the Wise; the Park of Eternal Glory in honor of the Soviet soldiers who were killed during the Great Patriotic War (WWII); the Kiev-Pechery Lavra, where . . ."

Laughing, the policeman said, "Stop! I've got you. You really are a tourist, not a businessman. You would have to be a Ukrainian or a tourist to know my native city so well."

"It's true that every other time in the Soviet Union I've been a student or a tourist, but this time honestly I'm here on an official business trip. You know the Russian proverb: 'The bitter truth is better than a sweet lie.'"

The policeman smiled saying, "I'm going to forget what's on your visa. I'm going to let a "white crow" go into the building for Construction."

The use of the term "white crow" was a compliment. The policeman was labeling me an unusual person, neither fish nor fowl.

"Many thanks!. All the best to you!"

All of the important sources for information I needed about per diem payments to workers were located somewhere in this building: the State Department's FBO, Fixed Base Operations, paying per diem to its employees, as well as three American firms, AegisConstruction Corporation, Continental Mechanical, and Circle Industries Construction.

It didn't take long to discover that per diem payments were secret. No firm wanted another to learn what it was paying its own employees. The easiest to crack was the FBO's schedule. The government's FBO now performed all the tasks to be turned over to the company winning the bid. In addition to salary workers received 20% of pay for hardship and an additional 5% of salary for cost of living.

After cracking the FBO numbers, I found getting information out of the private American companies extremely difficult. The most helpful was the project manager, F. Paul Griffith, of Aegis Construction Corporation who helped me during lunch. I found his office and his secretary on the second floor. The company was responsible for roofs, windows and insulation. After I promised to keep the data confidential and not to let anyone on the site have the information, she told me that the twelve workers received $750.00 a month for food. I spoke to the project manager of Circle Industries Construction, handling plastering and dry walls, who was fairly friendly, but would give me absolutely no information. The company was located on the first floor and his wife served as his secretary as well as the building receptionist. When I first entered the building, I chatted briefly with her not knowing the she was also the secretary of

Circle Industries Construction. I decided to come back later in the afternoon when I hoped her husband would be on the embassy site and not present at the office to try further to find out the company's per diem payments.

The project manager of Mechanical Continental Mechanical, located on the third floor was completely mum, no greeting, no farewell. As I talked he just looked at me, not saying a single word. The company with nine employees was responsible for all project mechanics. His secretary was sympathetic, but indicated her reluctance to say anything to me while he was around.

I decided reluctantly to leave the building and return in the absence of these two project managers. I feared that there might be a different policeman outside, but I was making no headway with the two bosses.

I couldn't get into the new site, but walking completely around it, I found some peep holes. My major discovery was sighting a huge abandoned leaking fuel tank lying on the grounds, far removed from the new buildings. I made a note to ask about this.

Returning to the FBO building, I saw the same policeman who greeted me warmly and waved me forward into the building.

The receptionist and Circle Industries Construction secretary greeted me warmly,

"I know what you want, but I can't give you much information. Various amounts are paid to each worker under separate employer agreements. My husband only knows his own and I am not going to reveal it."

"I understand completely and appreciate your candor. I probably can make a good estimate for Grace Industries without the information. I have two already and am going to try to learn what Continental Mechanical pays now,"

I climbed to the third floor and found the Continental secretary alone.

"I will tell you what we pay, if you promised not to tell my boss or let anyone here know about the sum."

"I promise."

"Continental pays each man $425.00 per month for food and recreation in addition to salary.

" I am most grateful. What can I do for you?"

"Nothing. But don't let my boss or anyone know that I told you."

"I won't. Again, thanks."

It was almost 4: 00 pm. and I hurried back to the embassy for the appointment with Mr. Beale.

Mr. Beale was cordial and apologized for making me wait all day to see him. He told me that an official visit would take place tomorrow at 10:00 a.m. with two competitors who have been notified at their hotels this morning. I had some questions.

"I notice that none of the American project managers now responsible for some construction areas know any Russian. Will the company who gets the contract have to have a manager who knows Russian?"

"We will insist on it."

"Will the company who wins the bid have to have made a site visit to the new embassy complex."

"The contract will not be awarded to a company which has not visited the site."

I already knew that the three American companies working on the site had a total of thirty workers. I asked, "Soviet Construction is the general contractor. How many Soviets are working on the complex?

"About 500."

"Five hundred? And no one seems to know Russian?"

"Knowledge of Russian is not critical. Each American company does its own specialized work and the Russian workers are involved in the all over construction without any American supervision."

"Thanks Mr. Beale for seeing me. I'll be back tomorrow before 10:00 a. m."

"No. Come at 9:00 a.m. Mr. Bernie Durgen is the acting FBO project manager. He will meet the three of you in his office before the official visit on the site."

Tomorrow, the 14th of August 1985, for me would be an unforgettable date in the Soviet Union.

Chapter Ten

A Pied Piper in the New American Embassy

Early in the morning after breakfast at the National Hotel, I set off for the American Embassy. Instead of walking, I entered the Marksa Prospekt Metro Station. As usual during rush hour all commuters were packed into the train like sardines. It dawned on me that I should have known better.   The cramped breathing space reeked with odors of alcohol and perspiration.   Many workers drank vodka before leaving for work and some even had a bottle or two to take to the factory floor.

To reach the embassy, I had to change to another metro line at Mayakovskya Station.   Traveling only one stop to Barrikadnaya Station was easier because I was propelled out the door with the exiting masses and did not remain in the car only to be squeezed even tighter in the jam packed car by the incoming mob.

What a relief to be on the street again. I vowed not to ride in the metro again during this visit, but later strategy changed my plans. When I arrived for the scheduled meeting with Mr. Durden, he informed me that he knew nothing about the meeting and was tied up.

"I have been informed by Mr. Beale that I had to have this meeting with you before I would have permission to enter the new embassy complex.. Can I go through the gate and enter now for my official site visit?"

"No. You'll have to wait until two other competitors arrive. They are due at 9:00 a.m. I'll talk briefly to all three of you then and together you will visit the site for a guided tour."

There was nothing that I could do, but wait in his outer office. No one showed at 9:00 a.m. At 10:00 a.m. I was losing patience. I insisted in seeing Mr. Durden again.

"No one has arrived. Can you give me a pass to enter the site?"

"No. You will have to wait for the others."

Finally at 10:15 a.m. one of the competitors arrived. Ten minutes later the second one arrived.

"I'm Nils from Frank Basil in Washington, DC."

"And I'm Alan from Holmes and Narver Services in Orange, California."

While we waited for Mr. Durden to appear, I asked them, "What kept you? Weren't you supposed to be here at 8:30 a.m?"

One replied, "Yes. My taxi driver drove me all over Moscow before getting me here."

The other said, "it's a long way from my hotel. It was a long ride to get here."

"Where are you both staying?"

"In hotels near Red Square."

"That's a fifteen minute ride at the most."

"I thought that the taxi driver may have been conning me about the distance."

Mr. Durden invited us into his office.

"Gentlemen, welcome! There is nothing much that I can tell you, but you will have an expert guide with you who will answer all questions as you tour the site. I have been here only a week and a half and haven't been able to adjust yet to this change in environment. I've been sick since the day I arrived. Let me introduce you to Mr. William Royer who is one of our contract electricians. He will take you to the complex."

On the way to the site Mr. Royer asked, "What are you carrying?"

"A tape recorder, a camera, and a clip board."

"The camera is not allowed in the new embassy complex."

"You mean that I can see everything, but cannot make a record of it for my contractor."

"Those are my instructions."

"You have a cell phone will you check on this again."

Mr. Royer call someone who confirmed the prohibition on cameras..

"Please tell whomever you talked to that if I cannot use a camera, I am leaving the group to appeal to someone higher up in the embassy."

We were now approaching the new embassy gate when Mr. Royer made the second call.   I was ready to surrender when the second call was answered.

"I am now told that you can bring a camera into the site, but must not take a photograph if I forbid it."

"Fine."

Not being an engineer, the tape recorder was far more important to me than the camera. I was prepared to record every word of explanation of Mr. Royer. He was a contract electrician who conducted every tour provided to the site visit contractors.

As we entered I asked him, "What's wrong with this huge fuel tank that I observed yesterday lying abandoned on the grounds?"

"It's not the only one. Fuel tanks have ruptured. We are now replacing them with steel tanks covered by fiber glass, which our construction contractors claim will not require galvanomic protection."

"How many Soviet workers are on the site?"

"About 500."

When we arrived at the housing area, I was surprised to see some units completed with all the appliances in place while adjacent units were often empty cement hulls. In the complex there are four housing units. Housing units 1, 3, and 4 have fan coil units. For example, in Housing Unit #2 in each duplex there are two fan coil units, one for each of the three bedroom apartment and a smaller fan coil unit for the one bedroom flats at the top of the three story building. I made a note that for maintenance in Housing Units #1, #3, and #4 there are a total of 123 fan coil units of various sizes depending on the space in each apartment.

Housing Unit #2 is the building for the senior embassy officials. It consists of the DCM House and 10 three story 4 bedroom row houses. Heating for these housing facilities are located in a crawl space underneath the houses. Each house has a multi-zone heating unit.

As we progressed during the tour from one housing unit to another, I stopped to talk with some of the many Soviet women working on the site. A little over half of these women were working independently and diligently without any apparent supervision in nooks and crannies of the complex. Others were sitting around with little to do. Almost all were middle aged. I struck up a conversation with one after another.

"Who are you, an inspector?

"No. I am an American visitor. What is a beautiful woman like you doing here in construction work? "

"Me beautiful. You need a new set of eyes."

Soon a crowd of women gathered. I was lagging behind the site visit tour. By the time I caught up with the tour at least 25 female workers were following me.

Mr. Royer asked, "What's going on?"

"I stopped to talk to some of the female workers and now a whole bunch is following me. I feel like Pied Piper."

"How were you able to talk with them? Do any speak English?"

"No. They speak only Russian."

"You speak some Russian? Well, I would appreciate you telling them to go back to work. We are approaching the office building."

"Ladies! Please return to work. We are going into this office building."

The female leader responded, "Ladies! Wow! We'll see you when you come out."

The building was the eight story Chancery. I later learned that on the site it was referred to only as the "office building."

Mr. Royer said, "We can view all the floors inside, but one floor is like another. Maybe a tour of the first floor will be enough."

The two competitors nodded.

"I responded, "I'd like to go to the top floor and see every floor on the way down."

"There are five electric elevators that are not working. We'll have to climb stairs."

"That's O. K."

The other two were not happy with my request. Even outside the building it was messy and our shoes were already muddy. It was obvious that both were interested in a cursory view of the building.

The top floor was bare, dark, and completely empty. The windows were installed and the elevator shafts appeared complete.

I asked, "Why aren't the elevators working?"

"The Otis shaft guides have been installed for months, but we haven't been able to get the elevators working.   It has been extremely difficult because all the material has to be carried to the upper floors on foot."

The seventh floor was like the top floor. On the sixth floor workmen were cutting out a beam which crossed upwards directly through the elevator shaft.

"What 's going on here?"

"The beam doesn't belong there."

On the fifth floor in a dark area away from the windows I saw some movement. After a moment or two my eyes adjusted to the darkness and I saw clearly two individuals, one wearing a hard hat and carrying a walkie talkie, the other a young very slim woman also wearing a hard hat.

"Who are these two," I asked Mr. Royer.

"The man is a seabee and the woman is a Soviet worker."

"What are they doing here?"

"The seabee is responsible for the security. I don't know why the woman is here."

"I thought that the Marines were responsible for security at the U. S. Embassies."

"Not in this construction area. As far as the woman is concerned, you must keep in mind that the Soviets are constructing this complex."

When we completed the tour of the building, we went underground to a labyrinth below the building. It was dank, muddy, and dark. There was some lighting, but the power suddenly went off for twenty minutes as we milled about with one flashlight in the darkness. This reminded me of the previous day when I was with Mr. Bullock, project manager of Circle Industries. He received an emergency call informing him that a transformer had just burned out in the Marine Quarters Building and there was no power. I recalled also that the power was off briefly when I was with Admiral Kurth.

I asked whether this was a frequent occurrence. I was told that voltage problems were damaging armatures.

In the underground basement, Mr. Bullock pointed out two emergency generators.

"These two 600 kw emergency generators generate 380 volts, 3-phase 50 hz and are run by two caterpillar engine units."

"I asked him, "Are they ever turned on?"

"They have been sitting here for five years and were turned out about that time."

"Since they have been operated several years ago, would the manufacturers warranties still be good?"

"I don't know."

This, I thought, was a large problem on the site. Much of the equipment in the complex was installed years ago. I was sure that warranties had expired.

"We have two boilers which are available to furnish hot water when the supply is shut off."

"Have they ever been fired?"

"I don't know."

The purpose of the boilers was to supply hot water when the Soviets terminated hot water for maintenance, as was the common practice throughout Moscow for a month usually in the spring or summer .

All throughout the tour, it was becoming clear that this complex was a hodgepodge of trouble.

Agreeing to Soviets' involvement in the project as the general contractor was a major blunder. It should have been known that Soviet construction was notoriously inferior. It took years for Soviets to complete the most uncomplicated building constructions. The quality of work had been so poor that the USSR brought in companies from Scandinavian countries to build new Intourist Hotels. The Prebaltiskaya Hotel in St. Petersburg and the Yalta Hotel in the Crimea are two examples of hotels constructed by foreign enterprises.

The procrastination, lack of supervision, and poor workmanship were obvious at the new American Embassy site. When I arrived in the summer of 1985, the project had been underway for over five years. The absence of supervision was clearly apparent when viewing the west side of Housing Unit #4. Soviet workers had intermingled gray bricks with red bricks to spell out "CCCP," the Russian equivalent of "USSR."

All construction was halted on Friday, August 16, 1985, my last day on the site. There are many reports of discovering listening bugs placed by Soviets as the reason for the work stoppage. Certainly the Soviet workers had plenty of opportunities to bug the embassy compound. The security gate in the summer was manned by inexperienced college students with no fluency in Russian. Security of the Chancery was not enforced by Marines. There was a general lack of supervision throughout the site.

Whether or not bugs were installed, the project suffered from other ailments which made it a disaster: ruptured fuel tanks, shoddy masonry work, poor welding, power surges, fluctuating voltage, and expired one-year warranties, and a lack of workman supervision.

Regardless of my view that any maintenance company would sink into a black hole, I was determined to outdo other site visit competitors. On the day of the official visit on the site, both representatives of competitive companies had been bamboozled by taxi drivers and arrived late for the tour of the compound. At the end of the day I offered to take them with me on the Metro to Red Square which was in the vicinity of their hotels. Both readily agreed.

"We have to change lines one time so watch carefully all the cyrillic lettering so that you can follow directions to the proper station when you return by Metro tomorrow."

One competitor asked, "Can you help me get a meal when we get back? No waiter in my hotel understands English and I'm having trouble getting anything to eat."

"My hotel is across the square from your hotel. Come to the National Hotel at 7:30 p.m. and I'll order dinner for you. By the way have you toured all the wonderful museums and other attractions in and around the Kremlin?"

"No."

"Well, you should not miss this opportunity in Moscow before leaving. In the Kremlin you can visit the Armory, holding a treasure of art and history. It contains the famous golden Cap of Monomach which was used in the crowning of all the Russian tsars up to Peter the Great, the first imperial crown of Catherine I, the coronation gown of Catherine II, a large collection of ceremonial carriages, precious stones, and a spectacular collection of Fabage Eggs. Don't miss also visits to the Cathedrals of

Annunciation, Assumption, and Archangel.   In the Archangel Cathedral insist on going into the deep cellar to see the 46 tombs of the princes and tsars, going back as far as 1340. Ivan the Terrible is buried there among the many others."

"It sounds like something I could do tomorrow. See you for dinner."

By 7:30 p.m. when the my adversary arrived at the dining room of the National Hotel, I had finished my dinner.   I told him that I had a well done steak with vegetables.

"Can you order the same for me?'

"Bring him what I had and also some ice cream for dessert."

I returned to my room to write up the day's embassy visit. For the rest of the week I never saw the other companies' representatives again.   Both were fairly close so I hoped that they spent the rest of the week together visiting the many sights in the Kremlin and around Red Square.

Again at the embassy compound, I was able to play the Pied Piper with a large contingent of workers following me. No one seemed to care whether they worked or not. The workmanship was so poor, it was probably a blessing that the Soviets amused themselves with me. Little did any of us know that construction on the Chancery would stop at the end of the week.

Despite the high hopes that Grace Industries would get the maintenance contract, it was awarded to another firm. Considering the sorry state of the complex, it was a hollow victory.   Two years later I walked around the site with two of the students on my summer study tour. The housing units were now occupied, but the Chancery building was still incompleted and the outside masonry worse for wear. I still had fond memories of chats with the following throng of Soviet workers(?) who made me feel like a modern Pied Piper in an Alice in Wonderland world.

**In foreground - National Hotel
In background - Intourist Hotel**

In foreground - Housing Unit #2
In background - Chancery

Golden Gate in Kiev

Senior Citizen Laborers

Taking a rest

If I only had some grass to cut

Sidewalk sweeper

Earning some extra money

Chapter Eleven

Shaking Tails

On occasion during visits behind the Iron Curtain I was tailed. In the early 1960s when I was assigned to the Soviet Army in East Germany as an American liaison officer, it was mandatory that I lose surveillance before carrying out operational assignments. These occasions were always in vehicles, never on foot. Exciting incidents with tails in East Germany are covered in my book, *Licensed to Spy* , published by the Naval Institute Press in 2002. Losing tails in the USSR was an entirely different experience.

One of my goals during my visits to the Soviet Union was to visit BABI YAR. In the early 1970's foreign visitors were forbidden to visit BABI YAR. Ten years later this prohibition changed and BABI YAR became a favorite stop for tourists on the Soviet Intourist schedule. Over this period BABI YAR also changed decidedly.

In September 1941 the German army arrived in Kiev. It was a welcome sight for the Ukrainians and Jewish population which had been oppressed and hated by the Soviets for many years. On Monday, September 29, 1941, a Nazi order required all Jews living in Kiev to report at 8:00 a.m. at an appointed location. They were told to bring warm clothes and possessions. The Jews thought that they were going to a train for deportation. Instead they were told to leave their baggage and were marched through a local cemetery to the ravine, known as BABI YAR. The ravine on the outskirts of Kiev contained a deep sand quarry. The Jews were lined up on the narrow ledge of the quarry. On the opposite site the Nazis emplaced machine guns to execute the victims who toppled into the abyss. The mass of bodies rippled like a wave, and those who were not immediately killed by the machine gun fire groaned and squirmed in the holocaust. German soldiers flashed their torches over the heap of bodies and fired bullets into those who appeared to be still living, but not before they checked to retrieve any valuables. Some soldiers violated any young women found alive and then stabbed them to death. SS officers finally ordered earth and sand to be shoveled over the remains. And then the Nazis were ready for the next delivery of human prey. On September 29 and 30 the Nazis murdered 33,771 Jews at BABI YAR.

The killings continued at BABI YAR into 1943. In an attempt to cover up the atrocity, the Germans dug up some of the victims and threw them into a bonfire. From then on they tossed even live Jews in the the fires. Mobile gas chambers were also brought to BABI YAR to exterminate Jews. Although the preponderance of victims were Jews, some gypsies, pigeon fanciers, those thought to be partisans, Soviet prisoners, and a few Communists and Soviet officials were packed into lorries and sent to their death at BABI YAR. All told over 100,000 were executed at this notorious site.

After the war the Soviets denied the existence of BABI YAR. A few brought up the need for a memorial at BABI YAR. The Communist response was, "Where they shot the Yids? And who said we had to put up a memorial to some lousy Yids?"

The USSR made three unsuccessful attempts to cover up BABI YAR. All failed miserably. One caused a flood of mud sweeping away houses, tram stations, and people. On the 25th anniversary, November 29, 1966, of the first executions thousands of Kiev residents flocked to BABI YAR . A few days later a granite placard was placed at BABI YAR by an unknown person or group. On the plaque was written that some day a monument would be erected there in memory of the victims.

In 1971 I read A. Anatoli's (actual name: Kuznetsov) uncensored and expanded version of *Babi Yar* , first published in censored form in 1966. Three years earlier I was privileged in New York to hear Yevgeny Yevushenko read his courageous poem, BABI YAR. I vowed to go to the site on my first to Kiev.

Arriving in Kiev in 1972 with an Old Dominion University study group, it was not possible to take everyone with me to BABI YAR. I was surprised that the tour guides look blank when I mentioned BABI YAR, denying its existence. At the first opportunity I asked Kiev residents on the street about how to get to BABI YAR, but only received shrugs of shoulders.

Persistent badgering of the tour guides finally paid off in an unexpected way.

With our group on a bus returning to our hotel at the end of the day, the Kiev guide approached me quietly and whispered, "We are going to get you to BABI YAR. Stay on the bus when we get to the hotel. We'll take care of your students at dinner. When the bus stops, get in my tour guide seat in front and the driver will drive you to BABI YAR. Tell no one about this!"

I thought, "What an opportunity! I won't have to worry about surveillance or losing tails. Also I can watch the route carefully and on my next visit to Kiev, take some of my students to BABI YAR."

We took off as soon as the last student stepped off the bus. Then came my first disappointment. The bus driver, a young man, said, "I'm going to stop by my girl friend's place and pick her up to go with us."

He drove a long distance through the city, winding down countless streets. I knew that this detour would dash any plans that I had to learn the way. It seems like forever before he came out of his girl friend's house. I was surprised to see both of them carrying bottles of wine and sandwiches. Off we went again on a half an hour's drive, eventually arriving at BABI YAR.

Leaving the driver and his girl friend on the ground, guzzling wine, I set about exploring the site. The ravine had been filled in. I found the marker which was said to be placed at the edge of one side of where the ravine was located. Extending diagonally across the words indicating that a future memorial would be built, was an large crudely carved X . For future reference to find BABI YAR during my next visit to Kiev, I was happy to note the close location of a tall communications tower.

After a twenty minute inspection of the undergrowth where I found a large part of the granite slab that someone had chipped off the placard apparently to destroy it, I was ready to return to the hotel. My driver and his girl friend were not ready to leave.

They had looked forward to this trip as a great opportunity to have a picnic. They both were disappointed.

"Let's go!"

"No way. We just got here."

"I've got to get back to the hotel. Drive me there first and then let your girl friend off afterwards."

As they entered the bus, the driver looked at me like I was the biggest spoilsport in the world. I tried to memorize the directions on the way back, but I was sure that the driver was prolonging the trip on back streets.

A few years later on my next visit to Kiev I decided to make a solo visit to BABI YAR. Our study tour was near downtown Kiev visiting a war memorial. The park was full of people attending a wedding. Following every move of our group, especially me, were two characters who, I was confident, were members of the KGB. I maneuvered in the crowd to a location across a cascade, placing them on the other side of the long stream of water. When they were directly opposite me, I photographed them and took off.

Sure enough, after I cleared the crowd and exited the park, I saw them trailing me from the distance. Although I had great success losing tails in a vehicle during two years in East Germany, I had no experience losing surveillance on foot. As I hurried to the nearest Metro Tsentralny station, on the Kurenevsko-Krasnoarmeiskaya Line, they closed the distance. By the time I got to the platform, both were right behind me. As the train approached, one was on my left and the other on my right. The car doors opened. A few people exited the packed car. I squeezed in, but only one of the two tails managed to push everyone in from the door and barely jammed himself into the car.

I stayed on the train passed two stops to Ploshchad Pochtovaya station, I got off along with my accompanying tail. Inside the station I crossed to the other side of the tracks to proceed back on a train going in the opposite direction. At the last moment I entered a car just as crowded as the first one. The tail was blocked by the throng still trying to get off the car before the doors closed. I was free.. When the train reached Ploshchad Oktyabrskoi Revolyutsii station, I was able exit and walk to the crossing Metro line, Svyatoshino-Brovarskaya, at Kreshchatik station.

I was on the line in the direction of BABI YAR. I left the line at Nivki station and walked north . After twenty minutes I saw the tall communications tower near BABI YAR in the distance. When I arrived, I found the site in the same condition as before. The slab with the inscription stood alone without a sign of change.

A few more years passed and I decided to make another visit to BABI YAR. This time I took a friend and member of the study tour, Ed Boone, with me. We had no tails. I was surprised to find BABI YAR completely transfigured. The only thing that I recognized was the nearby communications tower. BABI YAR was now a beautiful well-groomed park with an impressive statue..

A Russian group was listening to a Soviet tour guide describing the monument, "The monument symbolizes the courage and unbroken spirit of the Soviet people. You see before you the central avenue which leads up to a raised platform on which eleven bronze figures stand arrested in motion, In front is a Communist member of the underground, boldly looking death in the face with eyes filled with resoluteness and confidence in the triumph of the just cause. You see a soldier standing with tightly clenched fists next to a sailor shielding an old woman, And a young boy who refuses to bow his head before the Nazis as he falls into the death pit. Crowning the group is the figure of a young mother, a symbol of life's triumph over death."

What a crock! The Soviet guide's words were right out of a book for tourists. There was never the slightest mention of the Jews who were sacrificed by the tens of thousands at BABI YAR. The Soviets claimed that anyone who was not a Communist, soldier, sailor (What were they doing here?), mother or child was not a victim.

Why would the Soviets stoop to such blatant disinformation? The only answer is their inborn prejudice and hatred of Jews.

Now if the KGB thought that a foreigner was headed to BABI YAR, one could be sure that he/she would not be tailed. Loads of foreign tourists were bused to see the newly reconstructed BABI YAR and view the disgraceful untruthful misrepresentation of the horrendous murders of Jews at BABI YAR.

Although I never returned to BABI YAR, my fondest memory is ditching the tails on my second trip. It was a learning experience that stood me in good stead in subsequent surveillance. I wasn't pressured to lose the tails as was the situation in East Germany, but I kept my record intact. I never failed to lose a Soviet tail

Two KGB tails in the rear

BABI YAR

BABI YAR sculpture

Chapter Twelve

How to Avoid Claustrophobia in the Catacombs

The best advice to ensure avoiding claustrophobia in the catacombs is not to go inside. I had visited many catacombs, including those in Rome, but none matched the catacombs in the Kiev-Pechery Lavra.

Among the 11th to 18th century buildings in this monastery, the Lower Lavra contains caves, known as the near and far caves. After the year 1060 the church above ground became the center of religious life and the caves were turned into a burial site. For nearly 600 years these caves served as the monastery cemetery to inter monks, high clergy, and feudal princes. The unusual climatic conditions and caves' soil composition contributed to the mummification of the dead. The Far Caves are 280.5 meters and the Near Caves 228 meters in length. They are 5 to 15 meters underground. The tunnels' width varies, the widest being 1.5 meters. The height of the corridors also is irregular, averaging two meters. The overhead clearance in some spots requires a visitor to duck down to advance in this underground labyrinth.

In the early seventies I led an Old Dominion University study tour to Kiev and visited Kiev-Pechery Lavra. When we arrived at the Far Caves, we found hundreds of Soviet citizens, adults and children waiting their turn in line at the entrance to enter the caves. Our tour guide moved us to the front of the throng where several men chastised us for being placed next to enter the catacombs.

"Why are these foreigners given the right to enter without waiting in line."

The guide answered, "They are our guests from America."

"So what! Is this a reason for my wife and my children to stand in line for hours in the hot sun? We are citizens and you should not be allowed to take advantage of us."

"Shut up! You are setting a poor example of a good citizen to our guests."

All of us were embarrassed by the tour guide's actions. A few in our group decided to skip the visit to the caves. I apologized to the man who was most upset, but I proceeded through the entrance with the remainder of our group. The Interior was dark with only a few flickering candles for light. The atmosphere was the dankest I had ever experienced. The walls seemed to be very moist mud.

Soon we came upon bodies lying in niches beside the corridor. Their faces were covered by masks, which I was told later, served to conceal their hideous faces. In the darkness it was difficult to see the entire corpse and to my horror I touched the hand of one of the mummified monks. Believe me, I was ready to exit the catacombs as soon as possible. The Russians in back of us were pushing forward and we then were pressed against the people in front of us. It wasn't long before some of those in front of us expressed fear for their children's safety.

The next problem was claustrophobia, in front of us and to the rear. People began to panic, cry and scream. There was no way to get out. The flow which had been at a snail's pace now barely moved. Hours passed in the damp, dreary and frightful to many, eerie dungeon-like catacombs. We were packed in like upright sardines. Fortunately no one got trampled . No one could fall to the muddy ground. I kept my hands close to my sides to avoid another skin-to-skin contact with a mummified cadaver.

I joked in Russian with those around me which seemed to help those who were closest. After what seemed to be an eternity the narrow, jam packed line again moved slowly. To keep my own sanity, in my mind I compared the journey through the corridors to traversing the length of three football fields and kept my hopes up by anticipating an eventual crossing of the last twenty yard line before a slow motion advance to the goal line.

When finally we ascended and reached the glorious fresh air, I vowed never to enter these catacombs again. But I broke the vow. About ten years later the caves were again on our itinerary, not by request from me. The catacombs had changed decidedly. The route was shortened to twenty minutes. Now there was electricity in the corridors. The mummies were completely clothed with gloves on their hands. The journey was pleasant and leisurely.

The secret of avoiding claustrophobia in the catacombs was now obvious to me. Don't go in, or better, wait until the USSR gets around to renovating and modernizing thousand year old caves.

I took a little of the mummified remains with me during my first visit into the Far

Caves. When I looked at my hand in the light of day, I saw that I had some gunk on my left fingers. I wondered whether I had hand-to-hand contact with an ancient Kievan Rus chronicler Nestor or maybe another of the famous buried in the Lavra caves.

Chapter Thirteen

On Strike in the Kremlin

No one should visit Moscow without a tour of the Kremlin, the most interesting and attractive sight in the city. Most visitors enter through the Trotsky Tower, first erected in 1495. Inside one passes the modern Palace of Congresses, built in 1961, where Communist Party Congresses were held as well as a second stage for Bolshoi Theatre operas and ballets. The huge grand auditorium in the building seats 6,000. Passing by the 16th century Tsar Cannon, weighing 40 tons and with a caliber of 800 mm, making it the largest gun in the world, we enter Cathedral Square, the main and oldest square of the Kremlin.

On the north side is the Cathedral of the Assumption, built between 1475 and 1479, with painted portals framed with decorated white stone. The bright, spacious interior displays frescoes, paintings, icons, and chandeliers of unmatched beauty. Down under the cathedral floor is the burial place of the Moscow metropolitans and patriarchs.

On the square, near the Moscow River, stands the Cathedral of the Assumption, my favorite Kremlin cathedral. Built in 1484-1489, its nine shining golden domes are magnificent. Ivan the Terrible's Porch was added in 1572 to permit the tsar to observe the services, The Patriarch had banned Ivan from the interior because of his multiple marriages, certainly an indication of the enormous power and influence of the Russian

Orthodox Church. The iconostasis of immense historical value, contains icons painted in 1405 by Theophanes the Greek.

The Archangel Cathedral faces the Cathedral of the Assumption. It was built in 1505-1508 under the direction of Italian architect Alevisip Novi and combines early Russian architectural style with the style of the Italian Renaissance. Russian masters of the 15th - 17th century painted the icons on the 13 meter high iconostasis. Deep under the cathedral are the 46 tombs of the tsars before Peter the Great, going back to the oldest tomb of Ivan Kalita (Ivan Money Bags who began to increase the wealth of the Moscow princes). This Ivan died in 1340.

Dominating in height in the square is Ivan's Bell Tower. The belfry is a three-tiered pillar of octagonal sections, each smaller in diameter than the one below. Twenty one bells hang in the arched bays of each section. The white tower has a gilded dome which is in harmony with all the other glittering cupolas on top of the cathedrals. The height of the campanile is 81 meters. At the foot of the tower one can view the largest bell in the world - the Tsar's Bell. It weighs 200 tons. Beside the bell is a fragment, weighing eleven and a half tons which in 1737 split off during a fire.

Exiting Cathedral Square on the way to the Armory, one passes again the Cathedral of the Assumption and encounters the Grand Kremlin Palace, 125 meters in length. The magnificent 19th century structure has many ornate halls. Most impressive is the St. George Hall, richly ornamented with a decorative scheme dedicated to Russian army victories in the 15th - 19th centuries. St. George Hall is used for state receptions where guests can admire six bronze gilt chandeliers with

3,000 electric bulbs. Next to this hall is the octagonal St. Vladimir Hall which leads to the Teremnoy Churches, crowned on the roof by eleven gilded cupolas.

Next in view is the Armory, the first building one encounters when one enters the Borovitsky Gate near the Moscow River. By a decree in 1720 by Peter the Great the work shops of the Armory were converted into a museum. A visit to the Armory alone makes the long trip to Russia well worthwhile. It's a must see! It has one of the largest collections of fabrics and clothes in the entire world. Among royal regalia are the golden Cap of Monomach, used to crown all Russian tsars up to Peter the Great, the first imperial crown of Catherine I, and the coronation dress of Catherine II. Ceremonial carriages on display are unequaled in beauty and majesty. Countless showcases of precious stones and priceless gifts from ambassadors and kings are spread throughout the museum. The showcase of the best of Faberge eggs is a special challenge to anyone trying to find the most favorite egg. My choice is the Easter egg of gold, enamel, and precious stones given to Alexandra in 1899 by Nicholas II. It's an egg-shaped clock with a vase of lilies made of quartzite and diamonds. The egg is surrounded by a revolving belt studded with diamond numerals which indicate the time against a golden arrow.

Tickets to enter the Armory are required, so I made certain before departing the United States that tickets were arranged for all of our tour members. No visit to the Kremlin is complete without a visit to the Armory.

On one of my first study tours to the Soviet Union we had tickets to visit the Armory as the first venture of the day. As we passed through the Kremlin Wall via the Borovitsky Tower gate to the nearby Armory, everyone was excited about the chance to see the marvelous treasures.

At the door to the Armory we were refused entry. Our Soviet tour guard pleaded with the Armory officials to no avail. While we argued, group after group passed us and entered the building . The Soviet officials gave no reason for this denial. One Soviet only recited the Russian proverb, "A no is a no even to a judge."

I countered with the warning of an American action, "If we are not allowed into the Armory, right now we will go on strike for the day."

The Soviet Armory official was not influenced by this threat, but the Soviet tour guide became upset.

"What do you mean 'strike for the day?'"

"I mean that all members of our tour will disperse right now and not continue on today's tour schedule. Everyone will scatter here in the Kremlin and do whatever each wants until dinner at the hotel tonight."

"But the buses will be on Red Square to pick us up at noon."

"The buses will be on Red Square, but we will not be there."

The intourist guide then shouted at the Soviet official, "This is a disgrace! We got tickets. Let us in!"

With an arrogant expression the Soviet at the door, sweeping his arm in front of his huge body, waved us off.

I turned to the group, "Everyone take off on your own to view the many cathedrals in the Kremlin and then explore Moscow. If you have any reservations about being alone, pair up with those who know Russian. Anyone still concerned, accompany me. I 'm going to the USSR Economic Achievements Exhibition. It is the largest 'museum' in the country."

The intourist guide paled, "The buses will be here."

"But we won't be. We will be on strike until dinner eight o'clock tonight at the hotel."

Needless to say, our subsequent ODU summer tours of the Kremlin included swift entry into the Armory as scheduled. The Soviet Union did not want "strikes" of any kind and probably found even more undesirable - an unannounced throng of Americans wandering about the Kremlin and the city without accompaniment.

Chapter Fourteen

Puppy Love A La Russian

On every study tour an Intourist guide was assigned to our group. All were women, but this was the only similarity. Each had a different personality and work ethic.

On the first study tour of students that I took to the USSR, a ditsy blond who had never accompanied a tour joined us at the Moscow airport. The entire trip was like "the blind leading the blind." When we departed Moscow, the airport director was urging the police to arrest her for negligence which caused a delay in our departure. I interceded on her behalf. The final outcome of her fate was not divulged

Most reveled in the goodies that the group would give to the guide as farewell gifts. On this occasion the guide who had been efficient, but rather cool during the stay, treated the gifts as an insult, particularly because there was a pair of shoes among the booty.

"Don't you think that we have shoes in our motherland?"

I instructed the students to take all the presents and give them to the poorest of the staff in the hotel. These poor women shed tears of joy when offered the spoils. The first one who dove into the huge bag took the shoes.

During one of the tours in the middle eighties we certainly found out that there were shoes in the Soviet Union. This extraordinary guide brought extra fancy shoes to change on the bus on the way to the opera or ballet. She scheduled frequent banquets with vodka and caviar for us in nightclubs with floor shows. In the early mornings she sped to the hotel's beautify parlor for a hairdo before departing on our route for the day. She was always dressed to the nines and would fit in any day on Fifth Avenue.

I had my reservations about her, but everyone else loved her. Soon her expressed love for a young man on the tour became a challenge for me to keep the tour in a happy mood.

On every tour, at all meals and performances she managed to sit next to this twenty year old and gaze at him with moon struck eyes. He returned her rather harmless advances and often at the ballet or theater I noticed that they were holding hands. On this tour to the Soviet Union the young man's parents were present. They had traveled with me, but without him, in two previous summer visits to the USSR. The association seemed innocent and never advanced beyond hand holding until we had an overnight stay at Pokrovky Convent in Suzdal, an authentic 16th century convent that catered to foreign visitors. We were put up in very luxurious and well appointed log cabins. During the first night the Intourist tour guide tried to lure the young man into her cabin for sex. He rebuffed her.

To save embarrassment, I'll call the student, Tom.

The next morning Tom asked to speak to me alone.

"I had a bad encounter last night. Olga expected me to sleep with her in her cabin and was extremely unhappy when I refused her offer."

"She'll get over it."

"I like her, but no way do I want to get involved with her."

"Did you tell your parents?"

"Not yet."

"Well I'll keep on the situation. It will be best not to mention last night.

At breakfast Olga sat far away from Tom. She didn't have much to say to anyone. After breakfast she approached me with a sour expression on her face.

"We will leave after lunch to visit the five cathedrals and fifty churches in Suzdal."

"All in two days?"

"As many as we can visit on one day and then we go back to Moscow."

"I thought that we would be here one more night."

Pouting, she said, "One night here is enough!. Plans have changed."

Her decision pleased me because she would be out of her romantic cabin and Suzdal sights offered so much more than what we saw earlier in the week in Vladimir.

Suzdal was settled by Russian in the tenth and eleven centuries. The town of Suzdal was the capital of the entire region during the reign of Prince Yuri Dolgoruky. His father, Vladimir Monomakh, founded the large brick Cathedral of the Assumption and the royal residence next to it. Over the centuries more than twenty five monasteries, churches and convents were built in and around the rather small Suzdal fortress. The panorama of the fortress and churches with glorious domes and cupolas offers one of the most beautiful sights in Russia.

Olga was not interested in a group tour of the town so everyone proceeded independently. It was Sunday so Tom joined me and a few others to attend the services in the only active Russian Orthodox church in the town. The singing during the Mass was bone chilling and the experience was the highlight of the visit.

At dinner that evening Olga sat sulking with no interest, a sure sign that for the rest of the trip we would not have the near banquet-like dinners of past evenings.

We were to return to Moscow where if Olga's mood continued, not much Intourist money would support our good times. I spoke to Tom, "Can't your restore your previous relationship with Olga. She's like a woman scorned. Surely you are mature enough to smooth over her attempt to proposition you. Tell her about puppy love or simple friendship. Tell her that you love her like a sister. It worked for me once."

On the return bus trip to Moscow, Olga's attitude seemed to bring everyone down to her gloomy level. Dinner at the hotel was below par.

The next night we were at the circus. I had my usual front row seat. After the performance began I looked back to see where Olga was seated. Lo and behold I sighted her in the tenth row beside Tom. They were holding hands. Victory! At last we again would be on the banquet circuit. Tom had saved the tour.

Back at the hotel when I found Tom alone, I asked him how he had restored his relationship with Olga.

"It was the expression "puppy love." She loves puppies and thought this innocent love to be like that of friendly puppy dogs with no sex."

The next day we were back to normal - vodka, caviar, folk dancing.   Everyone was happy.

Upon our return to the United States Olga pursued Tom through the mail with greeting cards, notes and letters. Tom never responded.

Intourist expenditures must have been stretched to the breaking point by our tour's luxurious two-week stay in the USSR. No previous tour had come close to such luxury. Viva the "puppy love!"

Chapter Fifteen

Great Patriotic War Heroes

On most study tours we spent at least a half a day in Soviet elementary and secondary schools. One memorable visit was to a special school of English. The school was located in the posh Moscow Lenin Hills where the movie stars and ballet dancers resided.

The quality of Soviet schools seemed to be directly related to the distance from the center of Moscow. Those in the center were well equipped. Students were fully dressed in spiffy uniforms. Quality dwindled as location increased from the center of Moscow. Just fragments of uniforms appeared on the outskirts of Moscow. The pupils in the Lenin Hills school were dressed in clean, attractive uniforms. All the children were handsome. The main reason for their good looks was that their parents were the cream of the movie industry and theater.

Our study group was graciously received by the principal. We had to pass by workers who were busy on a large project, expanding and improving the front entrance. When asked about the work, the principal explained that the school was preparing the building for the next fall term. Later the children laughed at this explanation, telling us that the work began as soon as the word was spread that Americans were coming to the school.

The visit to this school provided an ideal opportunity for the community members of our group who spoke no Russian. Now they were able to communicate directly with the children in English.

Attending a class of third graders on Soviet history, we found individual children making reports about great Soviet heroes who fought in the Great Patriotic War (World

War II). After listening to two reports, I asked the students whether they had ever met any Great Patriotic War heroes in person.

"No. We read about them."

"You haven't even seen one Patriotic War hero?"

"No. Never."

"Well, right now in this room there are several Great Patriotic War heroes! I fought in the war as did my friend, Harlin Tillberg, who is standing beside me."

Almost in unison the pupils gasped.

"You fought against the Nazi beasts?"

The class was now out of the teacher's control. The children vacated their seats and rushed forward to grasp our hands.

One child shouted, "Tell us some war stories."

Harlin served aboard an aircraft carrier in the Pacific and related a story about a battle.

"This is not the Patriotic War," one pupil said, "Our heroes fought the Germans."

I then spoke about the fight against the Nazi U-boats.

"Defeating the U-boats helped the sending of military supplies to your gallant heroes."

"That was good."

"Together we tracked the Nazi beast to his den and crushed him."

The American hero of all heroes in the eyes of the children turned out to be John Lamond who as an army officer fought in the European theater.

A young girl asked the teacher, "Why can't we get our own war heroes to come to our class?"

The teacher answered, "This is a special school of English. Unless they come and speak English to us, we will continue to read and report on their valiant deeds."

Apparently war hero or not, an obvious higher priority was the study of English. The teacher valued our contribution in speaking English to the class more than our professed status as war heroes. Any Soviet war hero visiting the class had better speak good English or keep his/her memories to himself/herself.

Special School 5th grade class

Children of ballet dancers and movie stars

Class has begun

Chapter Sixteen

Get Out of My Store!

Old Dominion University Study Tour students were required upon their return to the campus to write an eight hundred word paper in Russian on a selected area of Soviet life style. Some wrote on the quality, quantity, and prices of available food in the stores and market place. Others wrote on transportation, clothes, morale, and a host of other subjects.

After completing the course some of their papers were submitted to competition in advanced level of the state annual essay contest, sponsored by the Virginia Chapter of the American Association of Teachers of Slavic and East European Languages. As result of the on-site research in the Soviet Union and excellent command of the Russian language, Old Dominion University Russian language majors usually won the annual prize.

Often I was summoned during the study tours to solve a problem or simply observe an usual situation that developed in the course of students' research efforts. Several come to mind about incidents occurring during investigation of the sale of Soviet clothing.

My daughter, Barbara, an ODU Russian major, researched Soviet stores selling women's clothing. Perusing the merchandise in one store, Barbara was attacked by a store employee who was furious when she observed Barbara jotting down notes about the quantity, quality and prices of dresses.

"What are you doing?"

"Just checking the clothes."

"No, you don't. Get out of my store!"

Barbara asked me what I thought caused the outbreak.

"She thought that you were a Soviet supervisor, checking on her department. A feeling of rage ensues when Russian workers sight a supervisor checking up on them."

Barbara was fortunate to find any dresses in the stores because the largest department stores often displayed beautiful gowns in the windows, but customers were disappointed to find only paper patterns inside for them to sew their own if the material was available.

Everett Martin, now an outstanding judge in Norfolk, joined our study group from Washington & Lee University. Everett was investigating men's clothing and sort me out one day to solve a puzzle he observed in one of the Soviet stores.

"Mr. Fahey, come with me to this store. Something is real strange. All the men's suits are the same - black, and the whole line of them are sewn together. What's going on?"

I accompanied Everett to the store and saw more than thirty jet black suits all in a row sewn tightly together.

"Everett, the suits are sewn together because the store personnel do not want any to be stolen."

Food was an easier research subject. One major, Nancy Afman, wrote a magnificent paper after many trips to the open market, state stores, and freelances on street corners. It was such a comprehensive study Nancy and I covered the topic on the local talk radio show.

There was never a dull moment while observing Soviet life style. Reaction like, "Get out of my store!," added to the sport.

Chapter Seventeen

We Want Our Samovars!

The greatest upset that we experienced during our study tour visits to the Soviet Union occurred with the purchase of four samovars in Kiev. Three students and one high school faculty member bought the samovars at a shop where second hand goods are purchased on commission. Thrilled with their finds, the students approached me before evening dinner.

I quickly learned that the samovars were extremely old and exceedingly large. These old samovars had been the mainstay and treasure of their previous Russian family owners. A dwelling was no longer a home in Russia without a samovar. If financial disaster struck, the last possession to be sacrificed in the home was the samovar. When the samovar was gone, all was lost.

Samovars are used to heat water for tea by means of a central chimney filled with coal. A tea concentrate is usually seated on the top. Many are made of silver, some of copper, and all old samovars are expensive items in modern times. Most Russian samovars are considered to be valuable treasures on a par with icons.

I greeted the excitement with obvious disappointment.

"What's the matter, Mr. Fahey?"

"Old samovars like original icons are considered to be antiques and the government will not let them exit from the country."

"No sweat, Mr. Fahey. We were given a certificate from the commission shop authorizing the purchase. We were told at the store to present the certificate upon departure from the country and we would have no trouble."

"No matter what you were told, I believe that there will be a problem. And how are you going to carry them from place to place?"

"We love these samovars. We will carry them on our laps."

Three of the samovars were extremely large and heavy. They were an extra burden in addition to luggage, but the owners struggled happily with their treasures, even embracing them on their laps on the flight from Kiev to Moscow.

During the five day stay in Moscow everyone on the trip visited the students' rooms to admire the samovars. Most thought, "What a bargain!" The price of the samovars ranged from ninety to one hundred fifty dollars. The value in America would be at least in four figures.

Departure from Moscow started off badly. For some unknown reason the customs officials forced Everett Martin to lay everything in his bags out onto the floor. They took their sweet time to inspect every single item. The plane's time of departure neared as Everett was finally allowed to repack his luggage. During this inconvenience all of us just stood around watching and waiting. At last we were motioned to approach the gate.

Suddenly we were all stopped in our tracks.

"Those samovars cannot leave. Drop them right there!"

"What do you mean? Why?," a student asked.

"Samovars are part of our motherland's antiquity. They are not permitted to leave the country."

I stepped into the fracas.

"I just saw a foreign businessman leave with one. What is the problem? These young Americans were assured when they purchased their samovars at a government commission shop there would not be a problem. Each has an authority certificate."

"That authorization allowed them to buy the samovars, but did not give them permission to take them out of the country. They stay here!"

Our tour guide tried to support us, but to no avail.

I tried another tact. "We are not leaving without them."

"Your plane is being held up. Now you have to go. We will give you a receipt for all four samovars."

"What good is a receipt? Are you going to return the money our visitors paid for the samovars?"

"Oh no! Your tour members own the samovars, but the samovars cannot be taken out of the USSR. You Americans can return to the Soviet Union and visit the samovars."

The Soviet official then wrote out a receipt and handed it to me. I crumpled it and threw it to the floor. Suddenly an official, elaborately dressed in a much decorated uniform, arrived at the scene.

The official screamed at customs personnel, "The airport is coming to a standstill! What going on here? Get these people on their plane!"

"Who are you?" I asked.

"I am director of the airport. Where is the Intourist guide?"

"Here's Svetlana."

"Place this Intourist guide under arrest. The rest of you move!"

Svetlana began to cry. I stood as tall as I could before the gruff director and said, "Leave her alone. She had nothing to do with this. You are at fault! You are taking property that belongs to our study tourists."

"I told you. Get out of here!"

Pointing to the Soviet tour guide, he shouted, "Arrest her!"

Realizing that nothing further could be accomplished, I started to move through the gate when I thought, "I'd better take that receipt with me."

Fortunately I found the crumpled ball of paper and scurried through the gate, the last one of our group to leave.

Back in the United States appeals for help to recover the samovars fell on deaf ears until I got U. S. Senator Spong involved. He was helpful in bringing the U. S. State Department into the effort to force the USSR to surrender the samovars. State Department representatives met with the Soviets in Moscow on several occasions, but the reports to me were always the same, "The USSR refuses to let the samovars leave the country."

State Department was very cooperative and patient with me and tried hard to convince the USSR to give up the samovars. Consul Robert F. Ober in the American Embassy in Moscow met frequently with the Russians about the samovars, but made little headway with them.

Consul Ober kept me advised, but finally wrote, " . . . It is extremely unlikely that this matter will be resolved in the students' favor . . . . "

Upon receiving this letter and becoming convinced that there were no more possibilities of productive meetings with the Russians. I came up with an idea - image. It's the one thing that the Soviets try to project to the world.

I sought the assistance of the Norfolk newspaper, THE LEDGER-STAR. I had a manufactured electric samovar that I had purchased at the Moscow foreign currency store for my son. I asked him to bring it to my house and invited those four who had given up their samovars to come at the same time. I also arranged for a LEDGER-STAR reporter and photographer to come to my house. In the living room the photographer took a picture of the four samovar owners hungrily looking at my son holding his samovar. The reporter used the photograph in an article with the unblunted message, "Give us our samovars!"

I sent the article to Consul Ober, asking that he present the article with photograph to the Soviets at another arranged meeting and advise them that I planned to have a similar article in the newspapers every single month until the samovars are returned to our tour members, the rightful owners.

In no time the State Department informed me the the USSR had surrendered the samovars.

On November 22, four months after the samovars were detained in Moscow, the final letter from Consul Ober arrived, " I was told today by the Embassy mail room that the four controversial samovars, which were packed by embassy employees were sent on the way to your Virginia Beach address . . . They will be traveling to Washington, by pouch, thence by regular mail."

In December the U. S. Post Office delivered them to me, collecting cash for the duty obligation. All of us had a joyous, tearful grand opening of the huge packages at the Old Dominion University's student center. The prolonged saga of the Russian samovars had a happy ending. Persistence and Soviet deep concern about "image" paid off.

Chapter Eighteen

Image

The samovar incident was only one example of how concerned the USSR was about her image throughout Soviet history. The roots of Russian deception in projecting a false image extend back to the time of Tsarina Catherine II when Potemkin villages were erected in cardboard to fool foreigners and conceal the real poverty in the area. Whether or not Count Potemkin used this ruse is open to debate among historians, but certainly the Soviet Union has employed similar subterfuge to deceive foreigners.

A prime example was the bricking over of priceless artwork on one of the cupolas of St. Basil's Cathedral facing Red Square to present a "spick and span" appearance of the Square in order to impress visitors to the 1980 Olympics. Unfortunately the major purpose of image was to wow the United States, but the effort failed as President Carter canceled United States participation in the 1980 games. Now when one sees photographs of Red Square or St. Basil's, it is readily apparent whether the pictures were taken before or after 1980.

During one of the two annual parades of heavy military equipment through Red Square, Kremlin towers and even Lenin's Mausoleum were badly damaged by massive vibrations. The enormous weight of the armor caused the cobblestone surface to sink four to six feet in parts of the Square. Red Square was closed for over six months to repair the damage. A high fence was erected around Red Square to partially hide the cranes, staging, and furious work on going for a half a year. Security was posted around the perimeter to prevent any photography of Red Square during this period. I bided my time to finally seize an opportunity to photograph Red Square from the GUM department store. The damage to the Mausoleum was so extensive during the parade, Lenin's body must have bounced like a rubber ball. USSR wanted no images of a crippled Red Square.

After WW II the Communists spruced up Stalin Allee in East Berlin. Hollywood type facades were placed to hide the unsightly buildings and rubble which contrast with the energetic reconstruction in West Berlin.

When we, Americans, arrived for a meeting with the Soviet military at the army's officer club in Potsdam, East Germany, the Russians asked us at the door whether we needed to go to the latrine. A negative response didn't stop continuous invitations during the meeting to break talks for a trip to the latrine. Finally to the Soviets delight, several of us had to visit the bathroom.

What a sight! The palatial potty was surrounded by velvet curtains and thick plush carpets. Ornate lamps graced the overhead. None of us had seen such opulence in a latrine. Several months later an East German defector informed us that he was one of those employed to remodel this latrine, costing seventy thousand marks. He told us that the decision was made as soon as the Soviets learned that the meeting with Americans would be held at their officers' club.

With about a dozen visits over the years to Tsarskoye Selo, one of Nicholas' and Alexandra's favorite palaces near St. Petersburg, at first I could not understand why during each visit I would find the palace's interior completely redone in a different elaborate motif.

Finally a supervisor of decoration cleared up the mystery. He said, "This is a major tourist attraction, now widely known throughout the world, especially since your American figure skater, Peggy Fleming, performed on television on the lake in front of the palace."

"I know the reason so much attention and funds are expended to show tourists this magnificent palace and gardens, but why every single year are enormous funds spent to redo entirely the interior decorations."

"You promise not to tell the authorities?"

"Of course not."

"As a state interior decorator this is my gig. I have the final say on the display of the interior's display."

"But why would you change the interior almost every year?"

"Have you seen the nearby beautiful town of Pushkin?"

"Yes."

"Have you seen other cities and towns in the Soviet union?"

"Yes."

"Now do you see why we redecorate the palace over and over and over?"

"No."

"It's because it assures our living in this paradise for the rest of our lives. It's the only job in the area and we don't want to ever leave."

How many other "image" projects are ongoing continuously to satisfy the desires of the work force? It could only happen in Russia!

Red Square undergoing major repairs

Chapter Nineteen

Drinking, Lying, Cheating, Stealing, and Bribing

Visits behind the Iron Curtain during the Cold War provided a small window into large domestic problems in the USSR. A larger view of Soviet ailments was provided in Soviet newspaper articles, letters to the editor, and the satirical magazine, KROKODIL.

I <u>Drunkenness</u>

Drunkenness has plagued Russia for centuries. It was not uncommon for children to have vodka in water glass proportions. The Soviet Union was aware of the problem and made a constant effort to fight the demon. Unfortunately drinking was a practice that was ingrained as a cultural and life style activity.

Attached to the Soviet Army in East Germany as an American liaison officer, I saw many examples of the seriousness of excessive drinking. Detained on occasion and accused of espionage, more than one interrogation was thwarted by drunken Soviet officers. I couldn't believe my eyes one day on the road in East Germany when an army fire truck approached, swerving back and forth from left to right on a narrow two lane road. We drove off the pavement just in time as the truck was barreling toward us. A drunken Soviet army driver waved wildly to us on the way past our stopped vehicle.

II <u>Lying</u>

Despite Russian proverbs upholding the telling of the truth, "The truth is brighter than the sun" and "The bitter truth is better than a sweet lie," lying never has been treated in the USSR or in Tsarist Russia as the grievous sin by which it is viewed in America. I used to kid Soviet officers, saying, "I am waiting for one time when I will catch you telling the truth." This comment was never greeted as an insult. Usually the response would be a chuckle.   The Russians whom I dealt with didn't take lying seriously.

III <u>Cheating</u>

There is a great difference in what constitutes cheating in America compared to the Soviet version of cheating. Time and time again I encountered this dissimilarity on the campus of Old Dominion University. When I chaired the foreign language department, a well educated Soviet immigrant enrolled as a German language major. In her thirties she had been a principal of a state school in the USSR. One day a contingent of the German class marched into my office with the charge that Marsha had cheated on a test and should be expelled from the university.

"What happened?" I asked.

The spokesperson of the German students answered, "She violated the honor code. After about half the class had completed the test and placed their test papers on the teacher's desk, Marsha went up to the desk and rifled through the tests, copying down answers."

"You personally saw this?"

"Yes and so did half the class who were still in their seats."

"Well, I will talk to her."

This reply did not satisfy the German students. "She must be reported to the honor court!"

"She is from the Soviet Union and doesn't understand. It's a cultural matter. Let me talk to her."

"You talk to her, but it was cheating and we'll take it to the honor court ourselves."

"Please wait until I get back to you."

I summoned Marsha. I approached the matter very cautiously.

"Marsha there is a practice here not to look at other test papers. The requirement is covered in the university's honor code. Make sure to be cautious about this in your German class and other classes in the university."

"Some students say that I cheated?"

"I know that you didn't intentionally cheat, but under the honor code students will look at copying from another person's paper as cheating. We all have to get used to things being different here. I told the German students that you had absolutely no intention to cheat and that should end the matter, but be careful never look at another student's test."

Marsha was not happy with me for the advice or my attempt to help her and the German students were furious with me for blocking their action to take the matter to the honor court and have Marsha expelled.

Unfortunately later Marsha looked at another student's test paper during a history examination and was expelled. Many years later I learned that Marsha had become a faculty member at an American university so I was relieved that she had learned our ways.

I realized how difficult it is for an American to believe that open cheating was a practice in the USSR, but Marsha was not the only example I can offer. I volunteered to help Russian immigrants learning English at the Virginia Beach, Virginia Adult Education Program. After their class ended each day, the Russian immigrants would sit at a table with me to conduct drills in English. One day a sixty-year old Russian woman ran out of the class, sobbing loudly.

"What's the matter?" I asked.

In between gasps, Tanya stuttered in Russian, "The teacher told the class that I was cheating."

I encountered the teacher at the conclusion of the class.

"I understand that you accused Tanya of cheating."

"I did. She was cheating. During the test she was looking at her neighbor's paper and copying answers."

"It's a cultural thing," I replied.

"It's not a cultural thing in my classes! I warned them on the first day of class that I would not stand for any cheating in my classes."

Efforts to convince the teacher that it would take some time for her Russian students to learn our ways and understand that classes are not conducted in the same manner as in the USSR failed miserably. The teacher could not understand that Tanya had conducted herself in school for decades with impunity in the USSR, the same way she had that morning.

Back with Tanya after my fruitless chat with the teacher, I said. "Tanya, let me give you some advice that you will understand. It's not allowed to look at others' test papers here in America. Here's my advice from a very popular Russian saying, 'Live with wolves, howl like wolves.' Follow that advice in America and you'll keep out of trouble."

IV Stealing

In the USSR the crime, stealing, was of epidemic proportions. This was not a Communist vice, but a cultural/life style problem. The Communist Party and the state press did everything possible to curb crime. It was a Russian predicament. I spent over two years in Communist East Germany and never had the slightest worry about stealing. After departing a German hotel, if one had left money in a room, one could be certain that it would still be there or at the hotel desk. In the USSR nothing was sacred, even when one was still present in a hotel room. Although one char women certainly was an exception to the rule as I will relate in the final chapter.

In the USSR the state fought all of these cultural failings with vigor. In the satirical magazine KROKODIL stealing was attacked with humor. In newspaper articles stealing was addressed as a major factor in losses in factory inventory. The cover of this book shows a Russian character depicted by KROKODIL in the 1960s up to no good as he enters a city park.

V Bribery

Satirical attack on bribery appeared frequently in KROKODIL cartoons. Bosses were targeted as the main culprits. The magazine paraded examples of administrative directors conducting all sorts of ruses to solicit bribes. Some turned their backs to the workers revealing a bank or slot, a device serving as a depository for the bribes. Each cartoon would offer a new subtle manner for inducing bribes.

The Communist government carried on an unrelenting crusade to overcome these domestic ills, but the long history of Russian culture and life style could not be reversed. All the social ills continued unabated throughout Soviet history.

Chapter Twenty

Farewell, Moscow

I would be remiss if I left my visits to the Soviet Union without addressing some of the strengths of the Russian character and culture during this Cold War period, especially after listing some of their social and moral failings, at least by our standards if not theirs.

I Compassion

I certainly had many opportunities to witness the compassion of the Russian people. Behind the Iron Curtain in East Germany no matter how angry Russian officers became during my detentions for alleged spying on their military, compassion won out in the end. As the cold Baltic Sea wind swept across the road where I stood by my burned up vehicle, a Soviet lieutenant colonel did everything possible to get me out of the freezing weather (See LICENSED TO SPY, Naval Institute Press, Annapolis, 2002). Several times on other occasions in the early phase of detentions, I suffered long periods alone without the opportunity or facility to relieve my bladder. I could always stand the wait longer than it took for the Russian compassion to kick in and relief was accorded.

Taking students on one Soviet Study Tour a few days after I had an accident that drove my head into my vehicle's windshield in Virginia Beach, Virginia, I arrived in Moscow still picking small pieces of glass fragments out of my forehead. If Soviet authorities acted in a harsh manner, I would dig out a particle of glass causing a trickle of blood on my forehead. Soviet compassion would immediately surface. Whatever obstacle confronted our group vanished. I found Russian compassion always to be more than skin deep.

II Appreciation of Literature

The popularity in the West of books by Chekhov, Tolstoy, and Dostoevsky obscures the awareness of the influence of Russian literature by Pushkin, Lermontov, Nekrasov, Gogol. and others has on the psyche and mind set of the Russian people. A vote taken in the United States to select the most popular Russian writer surely would find one of the first three writers mentioned above to be the number one choice. A vote taken in Russia would reveal Pushkin to be the popular choice. There are several reasons Pushkin wins the hearts of the Russian people.

Pushkin, the Father of Russian Literature, was the first to write Russian in stories using folklore, contemporary situations, beautiful expressions and words which introduced this rich language to the average Russian. The hatred Tsar Nicholas I openly expressed for Pushkin enhanced the love the people had for him. He had no peer as a poet in his day, nor do I believe Pushkin's poetry is surpassed today. Throughout the years children in Russian schools have memorized Pushkin's poetry. Later in adult life they are able to quote lines word by word. I found it to be extremely important in all my contacts with the Soviets, as an overt spy behind the Iron Curtain or a leader of study groups to the USSR, to recite when appropriate lines from Pushkin's poetry. Such a practice eased the bad mood of Russians I encountered on some occasions.

During my lifetime I have found only one former Soviet citizen who failed to recognize Pushkin as the greatest of all Russian poets.

In between two summer study group trips to the Soviet Union, the dean of the ODU College of Arts and Letters provided eight hundred dollars to sponsor a prominent literary personality for a campus lecture. At first I wondered how in the world could we find a eminent literary figure to come to the Old Dominion University campus for $800.00.

The Soviet Union had forced the exile of Joseph Brodsky whom the Soviet Union had branded as a "social parasite." In 1964 Brodsky had been sentenced to five years of hard labor. The following year the sentence was commuted, but Soviet authorities continued to harass Brodsky, denying him exit for international poetry forums, finally in 1972 forcing him into exile. After a short stay in Vienna, Brodsky immigrated to the United States.

In the 1970's Brodsky participated in a small speaker's circuit. Aware of Brodsky's problems in the USSR and his forced exile, our ODU Dean of the School of Arts and Letters, a former history teacher, authorized the payment of $800.00 for Brodsky to speak at the university. Brodsky agreed to speak for this small honorarium. It was difficult to fill the audience with the university faculty members.. Brodsky was an unknown to the majority of them. Even the dean decided not to attend and gave me the check to give to Brodsky after his performance.

Before Brodsky arrived, I learned that he had refused to answer any questions from the audience after his readings at another university. When he arrived, I asked him, "Will you allow our Russian students who are very proficient in the language, to ask you questions?"

He answered, "No questions. Where did you learn to speak Russian?"

"At Brown University and in Washington."

"You have no accent."

"Thanks. Although you won't answer questions after your recital, will you answer some of my questions now?"

"What questions do you have?"

"Pushkin is my favorite poet. How do you rate him?"

"Poorly."

"Really?

"Yes. You will understand when you listen to my poetry."

This may sound to be arrogance on Brodsky's part, but other than his surprising reaction to Pushkin, I found him to be friendly, modest, and even humble at times.

I did get one more more emotional response when I brought up the Soviet poet, Yevtushenko.

"You obviously are not a great admirer of Pushkin. What do you think of Yevtushenko's poetry? I met him at a national conference of Russian teachers in New York a couple of years ago."

Brodsky bristled, "He's a pawn of the Communists. The worst of all people."

I disagreed with Brodsky. Yevtushenko showed great courage in writing his poem, "Babi Yar," severely criticizing the Soviet government for hiding the massacre by the Nazis of the Jews in the Ukraine. This remark seemed out of character since Brodsky himself was a Jew. I felt that Brodsky was jealous of Yevtushenko, but I decided to let well enough alone. We talked about his reaction to people in America, his new lifestyle, and his future prospects in America, He recognized the great opportunities in our country and voiced strong appreciation for freedom.

Listening to Brodsky recite his poetry in Russian, followed by the English version translated by the American professor in his company, I thought the American who freely translated Brodsky's words, making them rhyme and convey even a deeper meaning, was a fabulous poet. Brodsky's monotonous chanting, I felt, diminished the performance.

After Brodsky was finished, I said to him, "The holder of your check is not ready to give it to you. We have more time. Will you answer some questions from our audience?"

"Where is my check? Who has my check?

"It's here. I'll make sure that you receive after a short question period."

With some reluctance Brodsky began to answer questions in Russian. He rapidly warmed up to the session and seemed to enjoy the lively banter.

After about twenty minutes of questions and answers, I said to Brodsky, "Your check is here."

"Where?"

Taking it out of my jacket pocket, I said, "Here it is."

Joseph Brodsky smiled and plucked the check out of my hands.

Many years later in 1987 Joseph Brodsky won the Nobel Prize for poetry. Four years later in 1991 the United States made Brodsky its Poet Laureate. No one was more surprised than I about Joseph Brodsky's amazing success. I also was not surprised when I learned that Brodsky resigned from the American Academy of Arts and Letters in protest over the honorary membership of the Russian poet Yevgenii

Yevtushenko in 1987. I will never forget the expression on his face years earlier when I asked him about Yevtushenko.

As much as Brodsky is admired today in America as well as in Russia where a memorial is planned in his honor in St. Petersburg, he did not have the slightest influence on the Russian psyche and mind set as did the other great Russian writers and poets.

III. The Magic Suit and the Honest Woman

I was ready to say farewell to Moscow during the year Brodsky won the Nobel Prize. My thoughts, ideas, philosophy and general outlook on life and people were diametrically opposed to the many deep thoughts, dreams and visions of Brodsky. I was in Moscow and was concluding my last trip to the Soviet Union. Gorbachev had already began movements that spelled the end of the USSR. My challenge was to get rid of a dear companion which stood me well in two decades of visits to Russia - my old business suit.

It was an amazing suit. It never wrinkled, even on 10 - 12 hour flights to the Soviet Union. I wore the suit on every departure and every flight home. Because of its wide lapels and an old fashion look, my wife would never let me wear it on other occasions. I looked upon it as a magical suit. Cramped in an airplane seat for hours on end, the trouser's crease would be as perfect as the day it was bought. No way could an unwanted rumple be found. Three days before leaving Moscow for the last time I decided to reduce the volume of my baggage, wear something else and reluctantly trash the suit. At the end of the day I cast it into the waste basket in my Cosmos Hotel room. To my surprise when I returned to my room late the next afternoon, I found my old faithful garment folded neatly on a chair.

Again, I threw the suit into the waste basket. The next day there it appeared again, meticulous placed this time on the bureau. I thought that I was destined to keep this suit forever. Early the following morning the room maid knocked on the door, entered the room and asked me, "Surely you don't intend to throw this fine suit away?"

"Yes. It's seen its day."

"Could I have it to give to my husband? He would love to have a suit like this."

"It's yours."

"Can I pay you for it."

"No. It's yours gratis."

"Bless you."

This was the day of my departure. What a great gift to me. A few hours before leaving Moscow forever, I found an honest Russian. But I thought again. Despite the cultural influences, KROKODIL'S badgering about lying, cheating, bribery, and other failings, every Russian whom I had met had been good to me. And not because I was an American. Often they mistook me for one of their own. I decided right there and then that as soon as I arrived home, I would cancel my subscription to the Soviet magazine, KROKODIL.

Farewell, Soviet Union! Farewell, Moscow! Thanks for the unforgettable ventures and sending me an honest woman to be a lasting reminder of a great people.

John Fahey and Joseph Brodsky

ABOUT THE AUTHOR

Professor Fahey served twenty years in the U. S. Navy as a Navy combat airship command pilot during World War II, operations officer and executive officer at sea, and Naval intelligence assignments. After retiring from the U. S. Navy in 1963, John Fahey began a second career as an educator. He taught for twenty five years, twenty two at Old Dominion University as an Assistant and then Associate Professor. He won awards as the College of Arts and Letters most outstanding teacher and the University's most distinguished faculty member.

He has served as a president of many educational and community organizations, President of the Virginia Beach Rotary Club, Governor of District 7600, Rotary International, President of the Naval Airship Association, and Chairman of the Board of Directors, Hampton Roads Educational Telecommunications Association (WHRO-TV, WHRO-FM, WHRV-FM). Presently he is serving as President of Old Dominion University Institute for Learning in Retirement and as a member of the Virginia Beach Mayor's Commission on Aging.

He has written three books, A Cartoon View of Russia, Wasn't I the Lucky One, and Licensed to Spy. Over thirty of his articles have been published in scholarly and professional journals, including Missiles and Rockets, Space Journal, United States Institute Proceedings, The Russian Review, Russian Language Journal, Conservative Digest, and The Torch.